BATHROOM
IDEAS THAT WORK

BATHROOM
IDEAS THAT WORK

Creative design solutions for your home

SCOTT GIBSON

The Taunton Press

The Taunton Press
Inspiration for hands-on living®

The Taunton Press, Inc.,
63 South Main Street, PO Box 5506,
Newtown, CT 06470-5506
e-mail: tp@taunton.com

Editor: Jennifer Matlack
Jacket/Cover design: Douglas Riccardi / Memo
Interior design: Carol Petro
Layout: David Giammattei
Illustrator: Christine Erikson
Front cover photos: (top row, left to right) © Mark Lohman; © Brian Vanden Brink, Photographer
2006; design: Dominic Mercadante, Architect; © Brian Vanden Brink, Photographer 2006; design:
Fixtures, Inc.; (bottom row, left to right) © Brian Vanden Brink, Photographer 2006; © Mark
Lohman; design: Lotto Design Group; © Olson Photographic; design: Sally Scott, Sally Scott
Interior Design; © Art Grice
Back cover photos: (clockwise from top left) © Eric Roth; courtesy York Wall Coverings; © Eric
Roth; © Brian Vanden Brink, Photographer 2006; courtesy Kurth; © Brian Vanden Brink, Photog-
rapher 2006; © Brian Vanden Brink, Photographer 2006

Library of Congress Cataloging-in-Publication Data
Gibson, Scott, 1951-
  Bathroom ideas that work / Scott Gibson.
      p. cm.
  Includes bibliographical references and index.
  ISBN-13: 978-1-56158-836-7 (alk. paper)
  ISBN-10: 1-56158-836-9 (alk. paper)
  1. Bathrooms–Remodeling. I. Title.

TH4816.3.B37G53 2007
747.7'8--dc22

2006017985

Printed in the United States of America
10 9

The following manufacturers/names appearing in *Bathroom Ideas That Work* are trademarks:
Adagio™, Armstrong®, Broan-NuTone℠, Corian®, Federal Express℠, Formica®, Kohler™,
Mannington®, MTI Whirlpools®, Porcher®, Sterling™

ACKNOWLEDGMENTS

I am grateful to the architects, builders, and bathroom designers who generously shared their time and their expertise to make this book possible. In particular, I would like to thank Carol J. W. Kurth, Cheryl Hamilton-Gray, and Mary Jo Peterson, all of whom went out of their way to explain the rudiments of good design. Thanks to Debbie Wiener, whose wit and common sense underscore a natural sense of design.

No book that relies so heavily on visual imagery would work without the benefit of many talented photographers. Thanks to Brian Vanden Brink, Eric Roth, and Rob Karosis, for their contributions and Sabrina Velandry, Eric's studio manager, for her patient assistance on too many occasions to count.

Bathroom products are available from many companies, and a number of them are fortunate to have knowledgeable and helpful staff. Thanks to Gary Uhl of American Standard, to the many product specialists at The Kohler Co. who took time to speak with me, and to Tiffany Hunt at Kohler for her many efforts on my behalf.

At The Taunton Press, I'm grateful to the very able book design department and to project manager Carolyn Mandarano and editor Jennifer Matlack for their thoughtful advice and hard work. Thanks also to Julie Hamilton, who had the thankless job of keeping text and photography organized. Thanks one and all.

Finally, I would like to thank my wife, Susan, and my children, Emily, Ben, and Molly, for their support and good cheer.

CONTENTS

Even the most carefully maintained bathroom eventually needs more help than a good scrubbing and a fresh coat of paint. Cracked plumbing fixtures, out-of-date colors, and just plain wear and tear all can make a bathroom renovation seem like the best idea you've had in a long time. You're not alone. Americans remodel nearly five million bathrooms a year, spending as little as a few hundred dollars for cosmetic upgrades like a new vanity countertop and basin to tens of thousands of dollars for a complete overhaul that includes upgraded fixtures, new lighting, and fresh wall and floor surfaces. As much as we seem to view our kitchens as the social heart of home, industry statistics indicate we're more likely to undertake a remodel in the bathroom: The number of bathroom remodels outstrips kitchen projects by nearly a million each year.

Bathrooms are among the hardest working rooms in any house, fulfilling both practical and aesthetic needs. Most of us will visit the bathroom at least several times a day. It's usually the first stop in the morning and the last at night, and it's one room in the house guaranteed to get a visit from your guests.

There's no single design that works for everyone or every situation. A basic bathroom must have at least a toilet and a sink, but these rooms can be shaped into highly specialized and personalized spaces depending on who uses them. Ever larger master bedroom suites often include proportionally sized bathrooms with amenities like steam showers, soaking tubs or whirlpools, elaborate lighting schemes, and floors and walls of exotic stone tile. But what works there is overkill for a child's bath, where the most practical layout may call for a basic fiberglass shower/tub combination and an easy-to-clean vinyl floor. A bathroom for an older or disabled homeowner is different yet, getting a curbless shower, sturdy grab bars, a wall-mounted sink, or a higher-than-average toilet.

Redesigning a bathroom to make it more useful or aesthetically appealing is at the heart of any remodel. But all of these changes take place in one of the most complex rooms in the house. A bathroom is an intricate system of pipes, wires, vents, and drain lines, much of it hidden behind walls and beneath the floor. All of its parts and pieces must be installed to specifications painstakingly spelled out in building codes that enhance safety as well as performance. While most of us could be persuaded to update a faucet or replace a toilet, an extensive renovation is serious work that requires both time and expertise. It may mean a number of specialty tradesmen—a plumber, electrician, carpenter, tilesetter, cabinetmaker, and plasterer or drywall installer—and possibly a designer to bring all the pieces together.

The sheer complexity of remodeling a bathroom is one factor affecting cost. Remodeling even a modestly sized bathroom can easily top $10,000. If that sounds too pricey, consider that a mid-range bathroom remodel consistently ranks near the top of the list in resale value, returning more than 90 percent of its cost. That outranks everything but a minor kitchen remodel and siding replacement— and is a better investment than a new deck, window replacement, or a new roof. Hundreds of manufacturers specialize in bathroom products that can be used to remake a room in any style, from Romanesque to Arts and Crafts or urban minimalist. All we need to do is learn how to take advantage of what's out there.

PLANNING

Before wading into the details of remodeling your bathroom, dream a little.

Great projects start with the big picture and that means taking a long look

YOUR

at the bathroom you've got. Ask yourself how it could

better answer your needs and reflect your lifestyle.

BATHROOM

The American bathroom experienced a transformation during the 1990s. What had typically been a small, functional room took on a new personality, and it began to play a larger role in the home. As kitchens continued blossoming into important household social hubs, designers also began to rethink the bathroom.

Larger houses have been part of the reason. Our houses are about one-third bigger now than they were 25 years ago, making more generous bathrooms possible. At the same time, our lives got busier and more complicated, prompting more homeowners to create private zones inside their homes where they can take refuge from work and family pressures. The idea that a bathroom can be a kind of retreat applies no less to smaller houses. A careful selection of materials and fixtures and a few simple changes in layout can make a comfortable haven of even a small bathroom.

A renovation can move walls to make the room more spacious, add new windows to let natural light flood the space, and make room for a deep soaking tub, an oversize spa-style shower, or a new vanity. But less extensive remodels can drastically alter a space, too. You can revive a fundamentally sound floor plan with new plumbing fixtures, cabinets, counters, or faucets.

Where to start? A good first step is to ask yourself a few questions: How extensive a remodel do you really want to undertake—a simple upgrade or a complete revamp? What changes can be made to better accommodate your lifestyle? How should the room relate visually and architecturally to the rest of the house?

right • Renovating a bathroom is an opportunity to change the focus of the room. Here, a large whirlpool tub and adjoining shower become the visual and functional focal point of the bathroom.

The Unknowns of Remodeling

Many bathroom remodels are prompted by outdated design and colors or fixtures that are just plain ugly. But there are other reasons to plunge into a renovation: design shortcomings, such as inadequate ventilation or insulation, and fixtures and surfaces that are simply worn out. Even the best materials don't last forever.

Renovating any room in your home is rarely as simple as it looks, and a bathroom is no exception. Early signs of trouble in a bathroom often include water-damaged flooring around the bottom of the toilet or spongy walls at the base of shower walls. You might even find more damage when walls are removed or when lighting is replaced. The unknowns can make it difficult to estimate with any accuracy just how extensive repairs will have to be. The best advice? Hope for the best, plan for the worst.

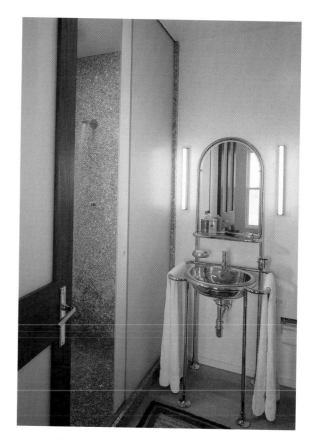

Bathrooms That Save Time

When you're on the run, catching the news or weather before work isn't always easy. If that's the case, installing a television in the bathroom lets you get ready for work and check the forecast at the same time. This LCD screen is incorporated into a bathroom mirror, putting the picture front and center when you want it and disappearing from view when the set is turned off. This television is only about 3 in. deep, so it fits in a standard wall cavity.

above left • Where possible, the addition of new windows will make a smaller bathroom seem larger while adding an abundance of natural light. The mirror on the side helps to reflect the light throughout this room.

above • Modern materials and fixtures bring new life to this bathroom. The separate showering area helps make the space a comfortable retreat.

Combining Design with Practicality

Many of us living in houses built as recently as the mid-1970s are starting with unimaginative rectangles that have equally unimaginative fixtures and components. But there's no reason a bathroom can't be more interesting and ultimately more practical.

Think about the overall impression you want your remodeled bathroom to make. In a home with an obvious architectural style, a successful renovation might mean updating the room without imposing an altogether different character. In a house with less obvious design roots, you may not feel it's as important to stick with rigid rules or any particular period look. Taking a chance can prove to be a lot of fun, so think of your bathroom as a design canvas where you can create a room that reflects your personal style. If you want a red bathroom, go for it! If you've always wanted a concrete countertop, this could be a good opportunity to have one.

Create a Clip File

If you're unsure what you want in your remodel or if you only have a few vague ideas, begin identifying bathrooms you find appealing. Flip through magazines and clip the images that catch your eye. Before you drop them into a large envelope or an accordion file, attach a sticky note to the back of each one with notations about what initially attracted you to that image. Was it the tile backsplash or the smart layout of the space? This exercise will help you be clear about your desires and also provide concrete examples to share that illustrate your vision.

Replacing worn surfaces and fixtures dresses up tired bathrooms. The simple arch-topped mirror flanked by a pair of wall sconces makes the vanity area the focal point of the room.

Warming It Up

There's nothing like a fire to take the chill off and set the right mood—especially when you're enjoying a soak in the tub or stepping out of the shower. Today's gas fireplaces start with the flick of a switch or a remote, making them a hassle-free way of adding warmth and ambiance to a room. With the variety of options now available, you don't even have to break into a wall to enjoy the beauty of a fireplace.

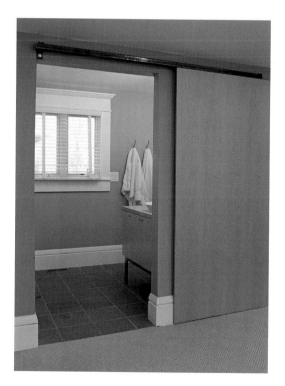

A remodel is an opportunity to rethink standard features and make a bathroom more practical as well as contemporary in design. This rolling door not only stays well out of the way when it isn't needed, but also provides an extra wide passage.

Bathrooms don't have to be just functional spaces. The large tub, updated fixtures, and decorative touches all combine to make this space practical and good looking.

This large bathroom has space for both a generous shower and a big tub located away from the toilet and vanity, making it comfortable for multiple users.

top left • Bathrooms can be more than utilitarian: A large soaking tub is roomy enough for two.

left • A curvaceous console table sink and a claw-foot bathtub add period charm to this bathroom. Empty wall and floor space is maximized for storage, which is typically lacking in both older bathrooms and those with pedestal sinks.

above • A powder room frequently used by guests is an opportunity for showcasting artwork and splurging on special cabinetry, countertops, or wall coverings.

Matching the renovated bathroom to your lifestyle means picking materials and fixtures that harmonize with your needs, tastes, and budget. For example, if you now have a tub but don't often have the time for a hot soak, replace the tub with a large walk-in shower and add a high-performance showerhead, which is something you can use every day. Lots of kids in the house? A bathroom with a one-piece tub/shower and a seamless vinyl floor makes more sense than a Victorian claw-foot and a wood floor. Empty nesters with room to spare might consider enlarging a cramped master bath by borrowing space from an adjacent closet or extra bedroom. In other words, let form follow function.

Exploring Materials and Finishes

Choices for bathroom materials and fixtures have increased dramatically over the last few years. Flooring, for example, still includes standards like wood, tile, and sheet vinyl, but to those add laminates, engineered wood, cork, and bamboo. The same is true of wall coverings, toilets and sinks, and faucets and showerheads.

This greater palette makes it easier to find the right materials and bathroom components that function well and also fit your overall visual strategy for the room. Wider choices also make it easier to have fun with colors, patterns, and textures. In a child's bathroom, for instance, bold colors and patterned wallpaper are certainly more entertaining than the plain white or subdued beige an adult might feel more comfortable with.

above • Mosaic tiles that line the walls of the shower have a tactile quality that helps to invigorate this small bathroom. Carefully chosen materials and surfaces show that varied textures and colors can be combined in a rich whole.

right • Brightly patterned wallpaper along with vivid colors in the countertop and floor give this kids' bathroom a sense of fun.

A Seamless Blend of Shapes, Color, and Texture

This contemporary bathroom combines different colors, shapes, and textures in a coherent whole. The blocky half-walls that define the shower have a sculptural quality that's enhanced by contrast in color and surface, from the blue tiled checkerboard wall to the long shower bench. Over the vanity, two circular mirrors help to balance the rectangular shapes of the light fixtures above and the cabinet below.

The bathroom really has two parts: a wet side for the shower and deep soaking tub at the far end of the room, and a dry side for the vanity. They're merged seamlessly in this design with a single sheet of glass that neither blocks light nor becomes a visual impediment.

above • A sheet of glass divides the bathroom into bathing and grooming areas without becoming a visual obstruction.

right • Materials make the room. This contemporary bathroom design relies on a sleek vanity, frameless wall mirrors, and large light fixtures. A brightly colored rug on the floor emphasizes the minimalist approach.

A Bathroom for Every Purpose

There is no single bathroom that's right for every home and homeowner. There are several distinct kinds of bathrooms, all of which have slightly different purposes and as a result dictate different levels of finish and different material choices.

A powder room, or half-bath, with a toilet and small washbasin is one variety. This room is often located on the first floor in a public part of the house—in an entry hall, for example, or in a nook near the kitchen—where it's convenient for visitors. It doesn't have a shower, so you can get away with using finishes and materials that aren't as water resistant as those that would be used elsewhere. If one goal is to make a good impression on guests, then this is just the place to splurge on dramatic wallpaper, a vessel sink, or stylish lighting fixtures.

Bathrooms for children don't have to be high style and in fact will do better with highly durable finishes and fixtures. Here's the place for a one-piece tub/shower that keeps water where it belongs, or for seamless laminate or solid-surface countertops.

A master bath remodel is where you get the chance to create a "hotel at home," a place where you can indulge your desire for more elbow room, a jetted whirlpool or deep soaking tub, and even amenities like a gas fireplace. Master bath renovations also provide an opportunity to increase accessibility for those with less mobility by adding wider doorways, curbless showers, and taller toilets.

top left · Function is typically more important than stylish colors and materials in a kids' bathroom. This one does the job well, with above-counter storage with open cubbies and undermount sinks that are easy to keep clean.

above · Because it's so small, a powder room is a good place to make a design statement, even if practicality is the overriding theme elsewhere in the house.

left · A remodeling project can preserve the grace and character of a period home, adding modern fixtures without rumpling the charm.

facing page · A large, walk-in shower can become the focal point of a remodeled master bath. Windows over the vanity and inside the shower keep all areas of the bathroom bright.

LAYOUTS

A key part of design is making sure the different parts of a room work together.
If you're building new or adding on, the bathroom is basically
a blank canvas to create the bathroom of your dreams.

THAT

If you're remodeling, you'll save time and money by keeping a bathroom
layout that basically works. Correcting major flaws may mean
moving fixtures, cabinets, and even walls.

WORK

A bathroom remodel can range from something as simple as upgrading a vanity or replacing a toilet to a complete overhaul, which includes the relocation of plumbing and electrical lines or even enlarging the room. Layout is a key consideration, not only because it has a major impact on what the remodeled space will be like, but also because it affects the overall scope and cost of the project.

There's no better place to start than with the bathroom you already have. Its shortcomings as well as the features you'd like to preserve can be a guide to what you want in a new bathroom. You might be lacking storage for linens, feel cramped when there's more than one person at the sink, or find there's not enough room around the tub to towel off comfortably after a bath. On the other hand you might want to keep the vanity sink for storage or the tub/shower unit because you have three young kids. Whether you work with a design professional or devise your own room layout, a detailed scale drawing will help you spot problems and envision design solutions.

The second step is to make a list of your priorities. Each major fixture comes with its own set of requirements—for plumbing and wiring as well as how much floor space it should have. What's at the top of your list? A whirlpool tub big enough for two? An oversize walk-in shower? A separate enclosure for the toilet or an enlarged vanity with two sinks? You may not be able to get everything, so rank your wish list to help make final decisions easier.

right • A bath remodel doesn't have to mean wholesale destruction of period features or fixtures. Here, those things preserve a sense of place.

top • A storage closet built under a sloping ceiling means welcome storage that takes advantage of the room's natural contours.

above • A ceiling of matching tongue-and-groove boards helps unify the room. Their horizontal orientation makes the room seem larger.

right · Simplicity is the key to this tiny powder room. Too much detail would overwhelm this space.

below · This bathroom isn't large but details like a wood storage cabinet, over sized shower head and naturally lighted shower make an impact.

Planning on Paper

Drawing a new bathroom on an existing floor plan can help you visualize new possibilities. This existing 6-ft. by 9-ft. bathroom is in a mid-1970s Cape Cod. It includes a fiberglass tub/shower unit, a single-sink vanity, and a toilet. By moving one interior wall about a foot and shifting fixtures around, a much more pleasing bathroom is possible, as evidenced in the after floor plan.

The window and toilet locations stay the same to help minimize construction costs and allow other amenities: an over-

sized shower that takes the place of the tub unit, a double-sink vanity, body sprays in the shower, new lighting, and a radiant floor heating mat.

What does the plan give up? Not much. A small hall closet was eliminated and some plumbing changes were made, but they were relatively minor and not nearly as expensive as moving the toilet would have been.

BEFORE

Bedroom closet

Hall closet

2 ft. 6 in.

1 ft. 1 in.

10 in.

3 ft. 0 in. × 6 ft. 8 in.

3 ft. 0 in.

2 ft. 6 in.

6 ft. 0 in.

Vanity 40 in. × 22 in.

2 ft. 8 in.

Scale: 1/2 in. = 1 ft.

- New flooring design with border and diagonal inlay increase apparent size of space.
- New double-sink vanity with built-in mirror above.
- New lighting, sconces, and decorative fixtures create ambience. Dimmer, fan, and heat lamp added.
- Linen closet eliminated; smaller door relocated and opens facing vanity and mirror to maximize open feeling.

AFTER

Existing wall remains

2 ft. 6 in.

6 ft. 4 in.

Wall-mounted faucets

Existing window remains with towel bar below

Toilet location remains

New stall shower with body sprays, hand shower, steam, and bench

Hotel-style towel rack above toilet

Bathrooms are probably the most complex rooms in the house. They have a network of plumbing and electrical lines, so typically the more extensive the changes in layout, the higher the project's cost will be. It may not seem like a big deal to move a toilet a couple of feet one way or the other, but relocating waste and vent lines is difficult and time consuming. Depending on how your house was originally built and where the bathroom is located, it may not be practical at all. Moving sink and shower drains is less daunting, but the job can still be difficult. The bottom line: If spending is a major concern, you're better off working with an existing plumbing and wiring layout.

Another consideration is whether you're willing to move a wall to gain more room. If there's an adjacent closet or bedroom that doesn't get much use, borrowing a few feet by relocating a non-bearing wall may mean a big payoff. In a house with a cramped second floor it may be possible to create a larger bathroom by adding a dormer.

Finally, you'll have to consider whether to gut the room or simply patch the walls, floors, and ceiling. In general, you're almost always better off tearing out and starting new. It will give your builder a chance to correct hidden problems and often makes the job go faster.

top • Small is beautiful: Colorful floor treatments, imaginative mirrors made from old window sash and a nice old claw-foot tub make this space comfortable.

right • The position of the fixtures was well planned in this remodeled second story. Painting the walls and ceiling the same color takes the focus off the shape of the roofline.

facing page • Creating a large bathroom opens the door to a number of design options, including the addition of a large soaking tub or walk-in shower that wouldn't be possible in a smaller space. It's one argument in favor of expanding an existing bathroom into an adjacent bedroom or closet.

Moving a Bath

The owners of this 100-year-old house in Seattle faced a dilemma: Their bathroom was on the first floor but their bedroom was in the attic. They wanted to bring those two spaces closer to each other and combine them with a laundry, but the existing floor plan didn't offer enough square footage.

Adding a dormer next to the master bedroom gave them a new master bath and an adjoining dressing room along with a compact laundry that disappears behind a handsome pair of cabinet doors. The plan didn't change the footprint of the house, but it made it much more livable.

A large bathtub, contemporary sink and vanity, and big curbless shower all have a modern flavor, but a beadboard ceiling, antique light fixtures, and salvaged schoolhouse blackboards help the bathroom seem at home in the century-old house. A dual-flush toilet and a heat exchanger in the drain line to capture heat that would ordinarily be lost made the project environmentally friendly.

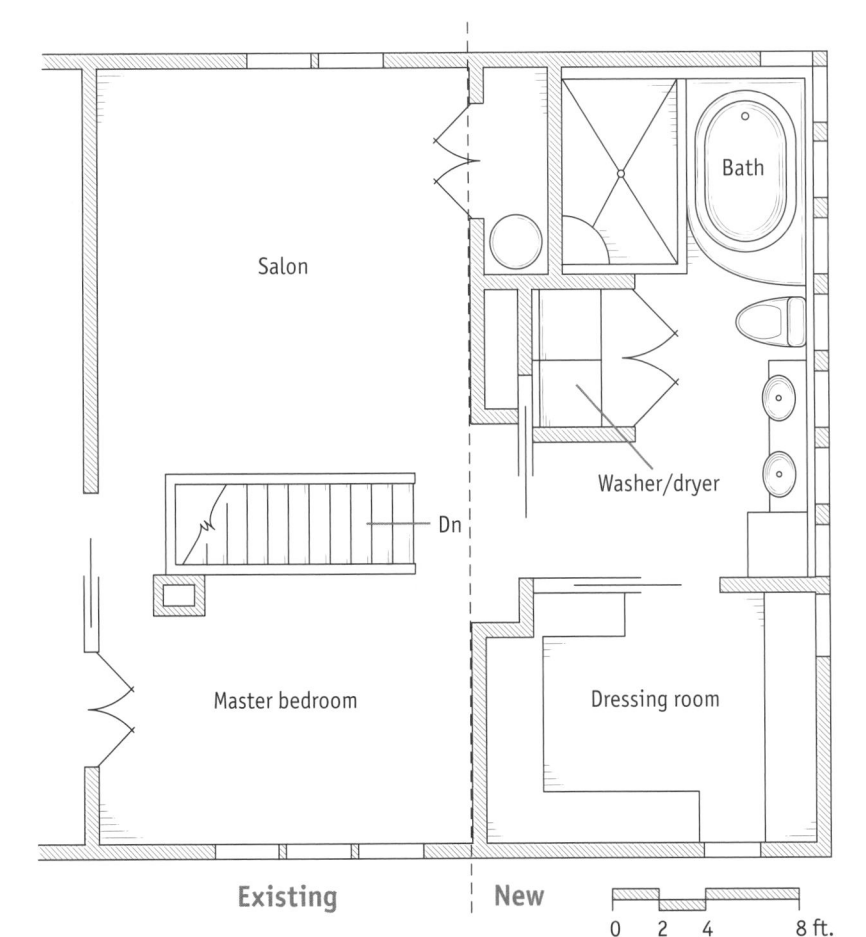

Salon

Bath

Washer/dryer

Dn

Master bedroom

Dressing room

Existing | **New**

0　2　4　　8 ft.

top facing page • **A new dormer helped turn a dark attic into a bright bathroom adjacent to the master bedroom of this 100-year-old Seattle home.**

right • **An efficient laundry is hidden behind a pair of doors, keeping the bathroom free of clutter.**

left · Charcoal gray grout helps to emphasize the green recycled glass tiles. They are set in white thinset. Towel bars are recycled aluminum.

far left · The backsplash was made from Pacific madrone milled from trees that had been downed in a stream.

Creating a Layout

Bathrooms don't have to be any particular size or shape to be successful. Part of the layout will hinge on how much room you have to work with, and part will depend on the plumbing fixtures and other room features you've identified as "must haves." For example, if a large whirlpool tub is at the top of your priority list, the rest of the layout should be planned around this major fixture.

A key part of design is the relationship of various room features to each other: the distance from a toilet to an adjacent wall, for example, or the clearance between a toilet and tub. These planning guidelines can be expressed as either minimums that meet the local building code or as design recommendations, which are usually a bit more generous. Both numbers are important for planning. A bathroom designed for someone with physical limitations has its own set of guidelines.

above right • This small bathroom is simple in style and decoration but the artful light fixtures and medicine chest bring the eye to the ceiling, visually enlarging the space.

right • A feeling of spaciousness abounds in this master bath thanks to a shower open on two sides, an open vanity cabinet, and gently sloping ceiling.

far right • If the bathroom has a single window, try locating it so it illuminates what you see when you enter the room.

Basics of Good Design

Every family's needs and every house are a little different, so rather than simply copying a floor plan you've seen elsewhere and hoping it will work in your house, make use of design fundamentals to help you develop a floor plan that works for you.

These elements were developed by architect David Edrington, who credits *A Pattern Language* by Christopher Alexander for many of the original ideas.

- Avoid layouts with more than one access door.
- Create an entrance alcove for a bathroom off a hallway to provide an added measure of privacy.
- A well-shaped bathroom is in the shape of a square or a rectangle whose length is not more than twice its width.
- Good bathrooms have a clear central area where you can wash or dry off, with fixtures like the tub and toilet located in alcoves around the edges of the room.
- Natural light is important. If the room can have only one window, locate it so it illuminates what you see when you first enter the room.
- Use the "intimacy gradient" in designing a floor plan by locating the most private parts of the bathroom farthest from the door.

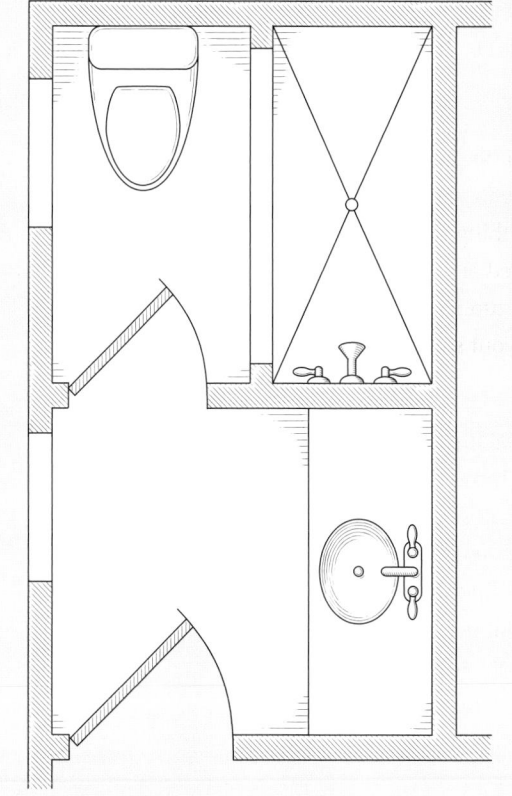

The Intimacy Gradient Applied to the Bathroom

The most intimate portions of a bathroom should be farthest from the door. In a small bath such as this one, compartments with doors do the trick.

An Entry Transition and a Central Space Improve Any Bathroom

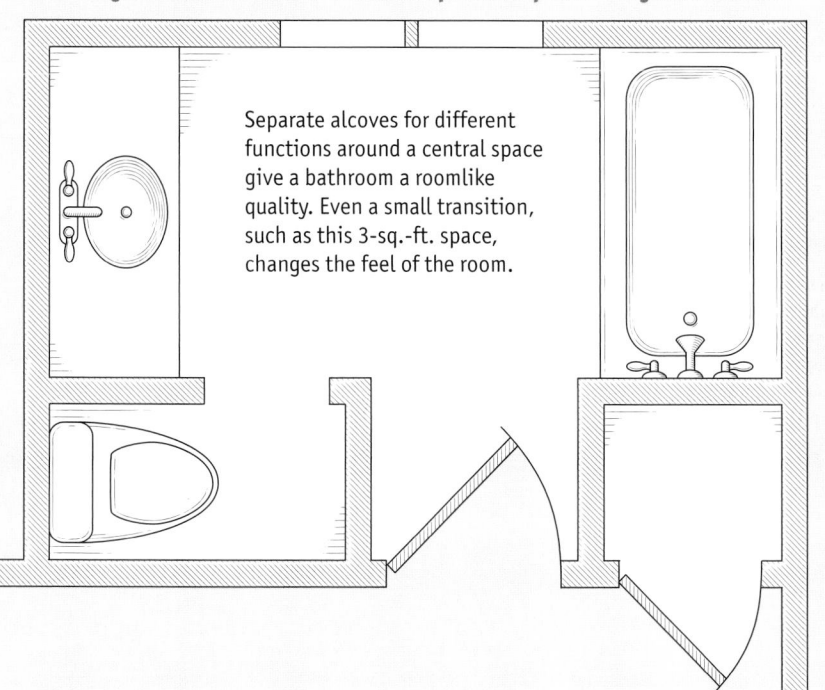

Separate alcoves for different functions around a central space give a bathroom a roomlike quality. Even a small transition, such as this 3-sq.-ft. space, changes the feel of the room.

Up and Out

When this house needed a new roof, the homeowner decided it was an opportunity to add a dormer and create a new upstairs bathroom. The dormer is only about 7½ ft. high, so the ceiling is sloped to keep the space from feeling cramped.

The components, fixtures, and accessories were chosen to keep the room feeling large and light-filled. A pedestal sink allows for more wall and floor space than a vanity cabinet would, and white subway tile keeps the walls clean. More white on the cupboard and medicine chest connect various elements of the room and leave a neutral backdrop for the black pencil tile that caps the tile wainscot. The design is enhanced by the 2-in. mosaic floor tile with a black pattern border at the perimeter.

One of the most carefully planned features of the room isn't obvious on first glance—it's the lighting. The room includes three different sources of light: rope lighting above the crown molding that introduces soft ambient lighting, wall sconces that flank the medicine chest, and a halogen spotlight in the wall near the tub for reading.

above • Bright tilework, an air-jet tub, and a vaulted ceiling turn this dormer into a spalike escape for homeowners. In-wall speakers and careful lighting design enhance the effect.

facing page • Sconces on each side of the wall-mounted medicine cabinet provide even light for shaving or applying makeup, whereas rope lighting over the crown molding makes good background lighting.

BEFORE

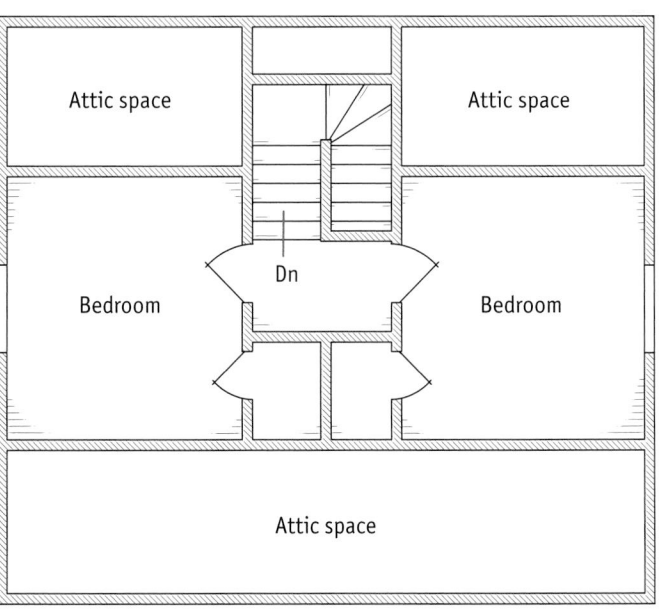

Attic space

Attic space

Dn

Bedroom

Bedroom

Attic space

AFTER

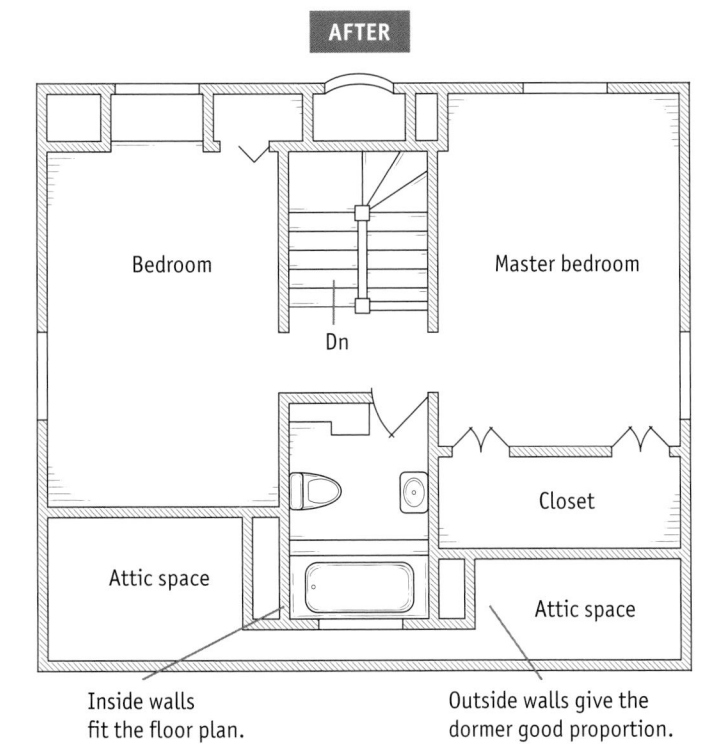

Bedroom

Master bedroom

Dn

Attic space

Closet

Attic space

Inside walls fit the floor plan.

Outside walls give the dormer good proportion.

You'll find plenty of sample bathroom layouts in books, magazines, and on the Internet. They can help suggest options for your own remodel, but because there are so many variables in room layout—exact dimensions, for example, or the location and sizes of doors and windows—you're probably not going to find a room that looks exactly like the space you're working with. Instead, using more universal design guidelines can help you adapt the features you want to the space you actually have.

Accessible Designs

A growing number of Americans are moving into houses they intend to keep well into old age, a trend that should lead to bathroom designs that are more accommodating to people with reduced mobility and strength. Having someone in the house who uses a wheelchair is another reason to rethink conventional bathroom layout and adopt the principles of what's called "universal design."

The idea is to make life easier for a variety of people—not just those with physical limitations or health problems. When it comes to designing bathrooms, there are a number of specifics that affect layout, such as increased clearances around the toilet, wider doorways, and a larger clear zone in front of the sink. Roll-in showers, built without a conventional curb, make it possible to get a wheel-chair in without hitting an obstruction. Some of these amenities are more complicated to incorporate than others—a curbless shower, for example, requires additional steps to keep water contained—but many are very simple.

Certified bathroom designers and builders who have had specialized training are good sources of information about universal design layouts. In addition, sample layouts are available by visiting the website for the Center for Universal Design, which originally developed these principles for accessibility (see Resources, p. 212).

above • The contemporary glass partition next to the shower door lets light into the space. Using the same flooring throughout unifies the entire bathroom.

COMBINATION BATHROOM AND LAUNDRY PLAN

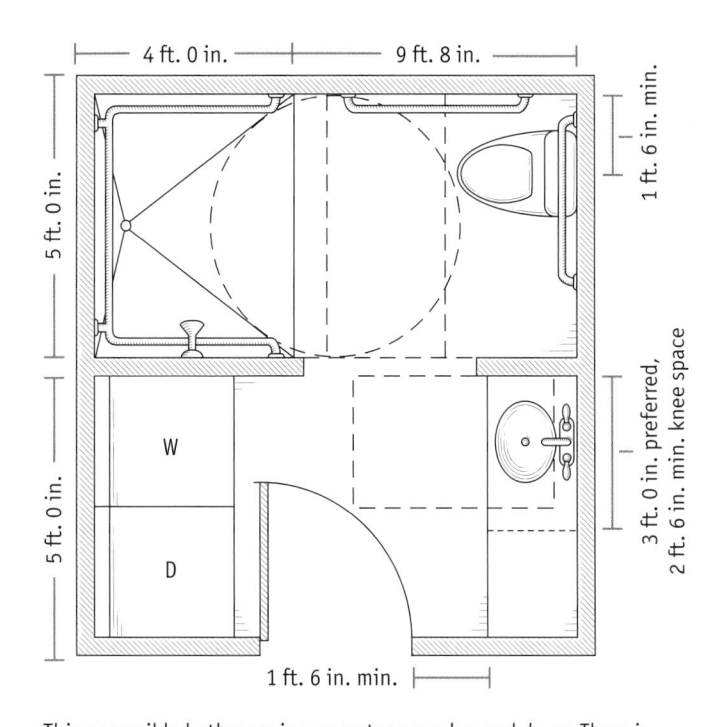

This accessible bathroom incorporates a washer and dryer. There is a 1 ft. 6 in. clear zone between the edge of the counter and the door opening. The shower measures 5 ft. by 4 ft.

WET AREA PLAN

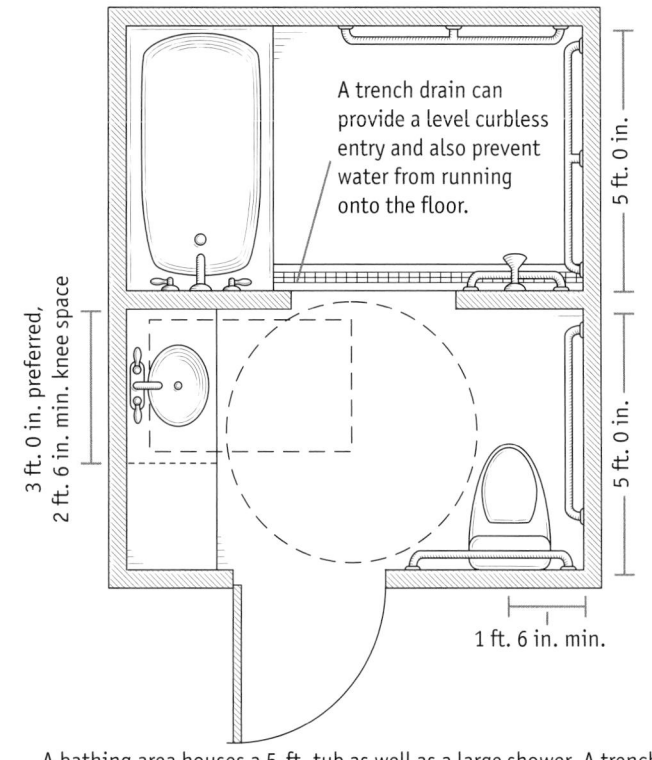

A trench drain can provide a level curbless entry and also prevent water from running onto the floor.

A bathing area houses a 5-ft. tub as well as a large shower. A trench drain at the shower door keeps water contained.the edge of the counter and the door opening. The shower measures 5 ft. by 4 ft.

ALCOVE PLAN

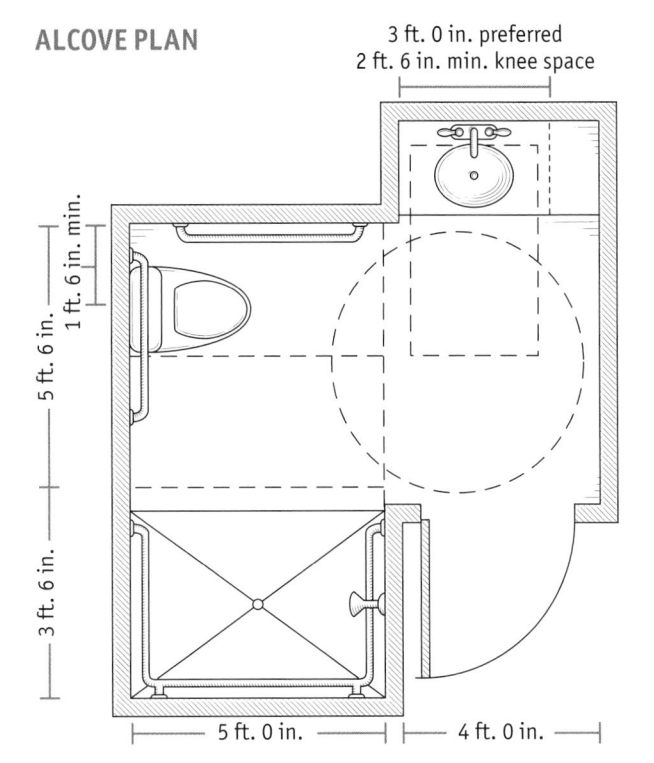

A bathroom door that opens outward should swing against a wall, not into the path of traffic. Inside, a knee space at the sinks measures a minimum of 2 ft. 6 in. The toilet alcove is 5 ft. 6 in. wide and the shower measures 5 ft. by 3 ft. 6 in.

COMPACT PLAN

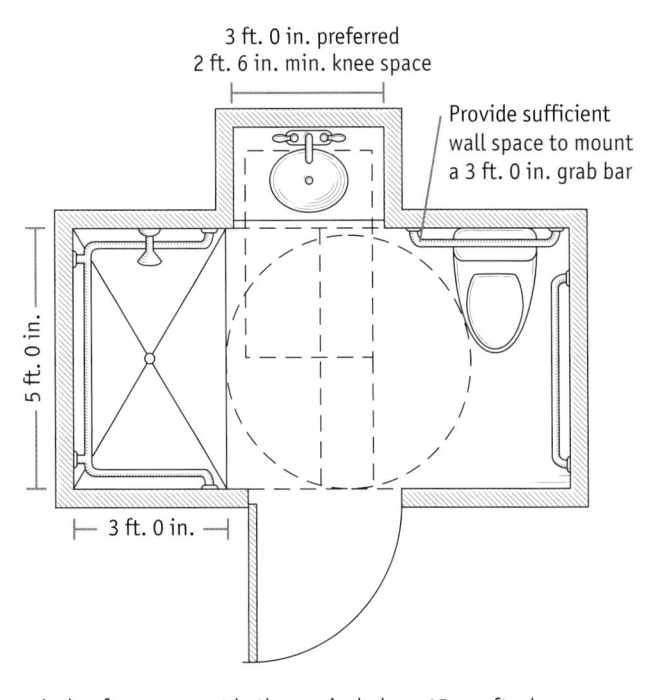

Provide sufficient wall space to mount a 3 ft. 0 in. grab bar

A plan for a compact bathroom includes a 15-sq.-ft. shower and a door that swings out to save floor space.

Hiring the Experts

Assuming you don't do the work yourself (not a good idea unless you really know what you're doing), you may hire both a designer and a builder. Hiring the right professionals is a matter of knowing what you expect them to do.

BUILDING CONTRACTORS

- General contractors (GCs) hire and supervise the work of all subcontractors on the job—carpenters, tilesetters, electricians, plumbers, and other specialists.
- Serving as your own general contractor may be tempting, but don't unless you have exceptional contacts with subcontractors in your area. Subcontractors respond promptly to those who give them lots of work, not one-time GCs.
- Ask for references and go visit jobs that potential contractors have completed.
- Ask the contractor to provide proof of liability insurance before work begins.
- Don't rely on the contractor for significant design work unless he or she has special training or there's a designer on the staff.

PROFESSIONAL DESIGNERS

- If the bathroom needs major nonstructural work consider a bathroom designer certified by the National Kitchen and Bath Association.
- Designers can suggest room layouts and fixtures and should be well versed in building code requirements and the principles of universal design.
- Fee structures vary by designer and by firm, but fees may be wrapped into the total project cost if you hire the designer to oversee the job.
- Interior decorators specialize in furnishings and surface decorations.

ARCHITECTS

- Architects usually charge more than bathroom designers, but they have a wider area of expertise.
- An architect will be able to integrate the design and architectural flavor of the bathroom with the rest of the house.
- Hire an architect the same way you would a contractor, by asking for references and looking at previous projects.
- Look for an architect whose overall style you like.
- Fees vary and can be a percentage of the overall project or billed on an hourly basis.

right • Today's fixtures and accessories are available in a range of styles and finishes so you can mix and match and still get a cohesive look, as evidenced in this period-style bathroom.

facing page • This bathroom works thanks to the use of a bold color above the wainscoting and contemporary lights set against a backdrop of traditional cabinetry and flooring.

Budget
and Timing

How much a bathroom remodel will cost and how long it will take obviously depend on the scope of the project. Construction costs vary widely by region, but a full-scale project that starts with tearing out old plumbing fixtures and taking walls and floors down to the framing could easily cost tens of thousands of dollars and take a couple of months.

Getting local building permits and developing a finished design are the first steps, and the design itself may involve weeks of back-and-forth conversations with the builder, architect, or designer. Demolition is usually fast, but the reconstruction process can be arduous. Even a straightforward project requires careful choreography on the part of the builder to get subcontractors on and off the job precisely when they're needed.

Setting a construction budget is one thing, but sticking to it is another. Be sure the contract you sign with your builder includes the overall cost of the project and specifies the intervals at which payments must be made. There are bound to be changes along the way—both design modifications and unforeseen problems once the walls are opened up—so a contingency fund of at least 10 percent of the contract price is prudent. Change orders should be handled individually, with added costs clearly spelled out before work starts.

Consider hiring a design specialist for all but the smallest project. His or her expertise may add to the cost of the project, but you're likely to get a better result. Keep in mind that no matter who you hire, getting the bathroom you want depends on both you and the builder.

Keep on Talking

Finding a professional you can trust is important in any remodeling project. Be willing to do your homework by asking friends or coworkers for their recommendations, seeking references from professional associations or trade groups, and checking references of builder candidates. Once you've settled on the builder or designer, go to the table prepared with your ideas about what you're looking for as well as your needs, what you're willing to compromise on—and not. Get a firm idea of how much time it will take to get your bathroom up and running. Open communication will help to ensure you get the bathroom you want in a reasonable time frame.

top · A contrast of light and dark makes this bath more interesting than a monochromatic scheme would have. A large mirror makes the room seem bigger.

left · Storage isn't limited to lower cabinets in this remodeled bath. Ringed by upper-level storage, the room can even house off-season clothing.

facing page · A major overhaul that includes a big tub and walk-in shower can easily take a couple of months to complete.

FIXTURES

*An upgrade to fixtures, from replacing a sink and faucet to
adding a walk-in shower, will breathe new life into any bathroom.*

Sinks

Bathroom sinks are unusually diverse. A generation ago the bathroom sink was by convention a white oval made to drop into a plastic laminate countertop, or it was a simple console table on slender chrome legs. Although you can still buy those old standards, you also will find sinks that look like washbasins, undermounts that complement countertops of natural stone or concrete, sculptural pedestals, and even sinks that don't look like sinks at all.

Not including cost, there are two key considerations in shopping for a new sink: what type of sink works best in your bathroom and what material it's made from. A good place to start your decision making is with the type of sink you like—a slender pedestal sink in a small bathroom if countertop storage isn't a concern, or perhaps a beefy console with heavy legs and a curvaceous deck in a bathroom with more space. In terms of aesthetics, undermount sinks won't dominate a room, but above-counter "vessel" sinks are often a visual focal point.

Beyond surface appearance you need to choose a sink for its durability. Cast iron and solid-surface sinks may not be flashy, but they will perform tirelessly with very little care. Stone and custom concrete sinks have a look and texture totally unlike glass; they also promise greater durability.

right • Twin pedestal sinks, each with a mirror and strong lighting for applying makeup or shaving, complement a his-and-hers bath design.

A Sink of Parts

Bathroom sinks can be expensive, which is one reason behind the design of this lavatory. It was assembled from inexpensive parts by an architect remodeling his own home. For about $50 he pulled together the aluminum stand, a basin, and a set of wheels (the sink doesn't actually roll). The result is an offbeat sink that pleasantly bends the rules and didn't break the bank in the process.

below left · Above-counter bathroom sinks, usually accented by wall-mounted faucets, may be reminiscent of old-fashioned washbasins, but they are among the most contemporary and fastest growing lavatory designs.

below · Pedestal sinks take up less room than sink vanities, but a supplemental shelf nearby may be necessary to hold toiletries that normally end up on a countertop.

Bathroom Sinks

Bathroom sinks, or lavatories as they're also called, come in a range of sizes and styles. What they're made from is a key consideration, as it impacts appearance, durability, ease of maintenance, and cost.

CHINA AND FIRE CLAY
$–$$

- Made by pouring clay mixture into a mold, then firing.
- Painted designs can be fired right into the surface.
- Hard, durable finish doesn't stain easily.
- Fire clay can be used to form structural parts, such as legs for console-table sinks.
- Simple china versions are among the most economical sinks.

CONCRETE
$$–$$$

- Can be cast in virtually any size and shape and dyed to any color.
- Inherently porous and will stain unless sealed; periodic resealing is required.
- Tremendous structural strength enhances design options.
- Significant weight makes shipping long distances impractical, so look for a local fabricator.

PORCELAIN OVER CAST IRON
$–$$

- Heavy and long-lasting.
- Nonporous, easy-to-clean surface.
- Available in several sink types, including undermount, wall-mount, and self-rimming.
- High-temperature manufacturing process produces high polish and deep colors.
- Abrasive cleaners can damage surface.

SOLID SURFACE
$$

- Nonporous surface doesn't stain and is easy to keep clean.
- Sink is glued to solid-surface counter for seamless installation.
- Many colors and patterns available.
- Minor surface flaws can be buffed out.
- Can be scrubbed with an abrasive pad without damage.

METAL
$–$$$

- A variety of metals are available, including stainless steel, copper, nickel, and bronze.
- Extremely durable but may require frequent polishing to maintain original appearance.
- Highly polished surfaces show water spots and scratches.

STONE
$$–$$$

- Wide range of colors and textures are available.
- Diverse material with a lot of natural beauty.
- Can be stained if not sealed; like concrete, may need periodic resealing.
- Extremely durable.

GLASS
$$

- Several types of glass are available, but tempered and laminated materials are strongest.
- Great variety of colors and shapes.
- High visual impact for guest baths and powder rooms.
- More likely to be damaged from impact than other sink materials.
- Some glass bowls susceptible to damage from sudden changes in temperature.

WOOD
$$

- Natural hues and variety of figure make material an attractive choice.
- Many tropical hardwoods are highly resistant to water damage.
- Resilient surface is more forgiving than cast iron, china, or stone.
- Finish needs repair if chipped or worn to avoid discoloration.

right • Self-rimming sinks, also called drop-in sinks, are a conventional design for a bathroom. They're often a bargain compared to the other styles on the market, but they're harder to keep clean than undermount designs.

above • Who says sinks have to be plain? Fire clay sinks can be decorated before they are fired, making designs and patterns a permanent part of the surface.

cause damage to the underlying substrate.

When properly caulked, the seam between countertop and sink won't pose any maintenance problems, but should that seal fail water can seep into the seam and

One disadvantage of this sink type is that the rim makes it a little more difficult to keep the countertop clean. There's also the potential for water damage.

Basic versions of this sink are still a stock item at most home centers and bath showrooms, but higher-end self-rimming sinks can complement even very formal bathrooms.

Self-rimming, or drop-in, sinks were at one time the most popular type of sink. Their simple form and low price made them the norm in most bathrooms, particularly those with laminate countertops, where the sink hides the edge of the hole in the counter-top.

SELF-RIMMING SINKS

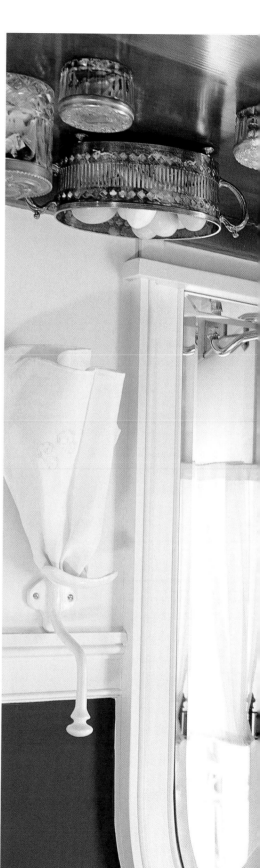

left • Self-rimming sinks can be set in tile countertops so that the top of the rim is nearly flush with the counter to simplify cleanup.

below • Sinks can be decorated as part of a whole-room scheme. Here, a floral pattern connects the sink with other elements in the room, including the toilet tank, the walls, and even the ceiling.

PEDESTALS AND CONSOLES

Pedestals and console tables combine the sink basin with a countertop. These sinks have at least two advantages over other types: They take up less floor space than a conventional cabinet so they don't crowd smaller bathrooms and powder rooms, and they're somewhat easier to keep clean than a vanity with a drop-in sink because there's no seam between the sink bowl and the top.

But their lack of storage is also their chief disadvantage. They generally don't offer much room for parking toiletries, and when this becomes an inconvenience they have to be paired with a nearby cupboard, a medicine chest, or even a broad shelf on the wall.

Both types come in a variety of contemporary and traditional styles, and in several heights and bowl sizes. Although basic pedestals can be among the least expensive options for a bathroom sink, high-end console tables that combine a glass bowl and table can be extremely pricey. Like bathroom vanities, pedestal sinks and console tables are now available in heights that approach the kitchen counter standard of 36 in., making them much more comfortable for taller people.

top right • Pedestal sinks are available in striking modern designs that complement contemporary house designs.

top left • Console sinks can have an appealing period flavor that complements an older home. The integral towel bars on this sink also are decidedly useful.

right • Console tables come in more than one style and can be muscular in style just as easily as delicate. Manufacturers also are more likely to offer consoles and vanities that are higher than the old norm, making them more comfortable to use, particularly for tall people.

facing page • This marble console sink matches the tub surround. With an undermount sink and easy-to-clean chrome legs, it's a practical as well as attractive choice.

UNDERMOUNTS

Undermount sinks have a seamless, contemporary look, and they have at least one practical advantage over conventional self-rimming sinks: Counters can be swept clean without worrying about a protruding lip.

Undermount sinks are often a more expensive option than self-rimming sinks, however, and they are not compatible with all countertop materials. There's no practical way, for example, of joining a plastic laminate top and an undermount sink because the raw edges of the particleboard or plywood countertop substrate would be left exposed. If, on the other hand, the countertop is concrete or solid surfacing, sink and counter can be made as one, completely eliminating the seam.

top · This undermount sink set in a marble counter contributes to the clean lines of this furniture-like vanity.

right · Undermount sinks are a perfect complement to stone countertops, in part because the exposed edges of the counter material are not susceptible to water damage.

Casting Concrete Counters

Concrete's inherent versatility is an opportunity for homeowner, builder, and concrete fabricator to collaborate on a unique installation, such as this two-bowl countertop in the master bath of a Martha's Vineyard, Mass., home.

Everything from the countertop thickness to the shape of the bowls and the color of the concrete was planned to fit this space and complement colors and textures elsewhere in the room. This counter cost about the same as natural stone yet offers many design advantages.

Concrete has become increasingly popular and many more fabricators are available to install it, but an experienced professional is key to create the right look based on the design approach of the room.

top • For about the same cost as stone, these homeowners opted for a custom concrete countertop that could be shaped, colored, and textured to fit the room.

left • With minimalist features and very even color tones, the concrete countertop in this bathroom stands out as a focal point, particularly because it's long enough to accommodate two sink bowls.

WALL-MOUNTED SINKS

Wall-mounted sinks are available in surprising variety, from massive antique fixtures with integral backsplashes to elegant wood sinks made for very contemporary settings. These sinks have the same advantage as pedestals in that they don't take up very much floor space, and they make cleaning even easier because there's nothing on the floor to interfere with a mop or broom. Wall-mounted sinks also share the major weakness of pedestals and console tables—a lack of room for toiletries. They also require substantial bracing. If you decide you want one, even walls that are in very good shape will have to be disassembled during a remodel so additional framing can be installed.

above • Wall-mounted sinks are available in a variety of designs, like this one that could have been inspired by a Salvador Dalí painting.

top right • Although not enormously practical given their lack of storage space, a wall-mounted sink provides an opportunity to make a statement, like this high-end wood vessel.

right • This glass counter and sink supported by unobtrusive wall brackets was pricey, but it takes up no floor space and reflects the natural light from the windows, making the room brighter.

Facing page • This sturdy wall-mounted sink looks right at home in a period bathroom, but its weight also requires extra wall bracing that isn't necessary with other sink styles.

right • Above-counter sinks are popular, but they have more exposed surface area to keep clean than conventional designs.

top right • Massive and thick-walled, this sink lends visual weight to the bathroom. The wall-mounted faucet, tile countertop, and tile banding around the room make the color and texture stand out.

above • This chunky above-counter sink complements the rectangular block pattern of wall brick and the extra-thick countertop in this bathroom.

ABOVE-COUNTER SINKS

Above-counter sinks are more commonly known as "vessel sinks" (a Kohler Co. trademark), and have a resemblance to washbasins that sat on bureaus in the days before modern bathrooms. Vessel sinks are made in various materials, from vitreous china to bronze and glass, and thus range considerably in price.

The beauty of a vessel sink is that it's so dramatic, making it a powerful design element in any bathroom. Because its edges stand well above counter height, though, this type of sink may not seem so handy in actual use. And whereas the materials used to make these sinks are often stronger than they look, thin, exposed edges will be more susceptible to damage than sinks that are reinforced by a countertop.

Wall Faucets

Faucets that emerge from the wall behind a sink have a sleek, built-in look, but be prepared for extra cost and the need for careful planning. Your plumber will have to know the exact height and location of the sink early in the remodeling process so water lines can be installed accurately. In addition, burying supply lines in outside walls increases the chance of a midwinter freeze and broken water lines.

left • Faucets that pop out of the wall above a sink are growing in popularity. The spoutlike faucet style brings the water close to the sink, meaning less splash around the bowl area.

More Sink Options

Bathroom sinks can be more than a familiar white oval made from vitreous china. Manufacturers are more inventive than ever when it comes to offering a variety of sink shapes and materials. In addition to traditional designs with classic detailing, you'll find everything from nearly flat traylike sinks to hand-blown glass vessels.

1. The simplicity of this washbasin-like sink with a wall-mounted faucet set on a slab countertop gives this bathroom an uncluttered, minimalist feel.
2. With its heavy, curving legs and thick countertop, this console sink is a major visual element in the bathroom. **3.** These sinks combine the beauty of the above-counter style with the practicality of a self-rimming design.

4. The very shallow bowl of this sink works well with a faucet emptying directly into the drain to minimize splashing. 5. The simple lines and classic shape of this pedestal sink will never go out of style. 6. A one-piece sink and countertop is easy to keep clean, and the integral backsplash keeps water where it belongs.

Countertops

Countertops play an important supporting role in the bathroom. They don't have a mechanical function like a faucet or toilet, but they make a big visual contribution to the room. Beyond that, a countertop must meet certain practical requirements—resistance to stains, water, and wear chief among them. There is a fairly long list of materials that fits the bill, available in many colors, patterns, and price ranges, including options you might not have thought of.

above • The roughened edge of this natural stone counter and backsplash add to the contemporary feel of this sink.

right • Ceramic tile comes in a variety of shapes, colors, and textures, making it a flexible and attractive material for countertops. The wide white grout lines in this design bring attention to the tilework but should be sealed to prevent staining.

DETAILS THAT WORK

Using Found Materials

Mosaics of broken pottery can make durable, attractive, and offbeat countertops. The technique is called "pique assiette." It's essentially a tiled surface, except the bits of china or pottery are more irregular. Raw materials cost next to nothing, but assembling all those pieces can be a painstakingly slow process.

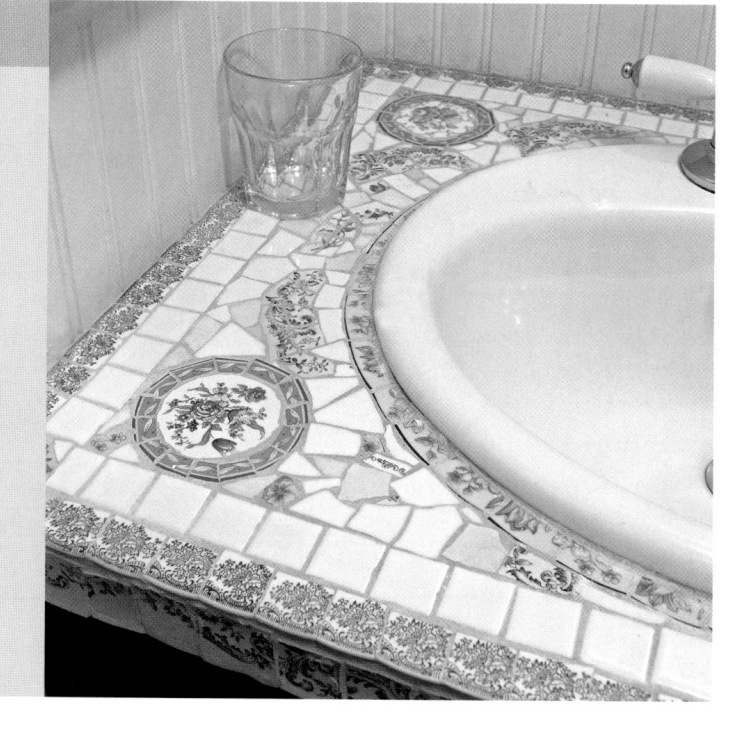

below • This granite countertop blends nicely with the wood tones and translucent glass doors. The wall mirror contributes to the spare design.

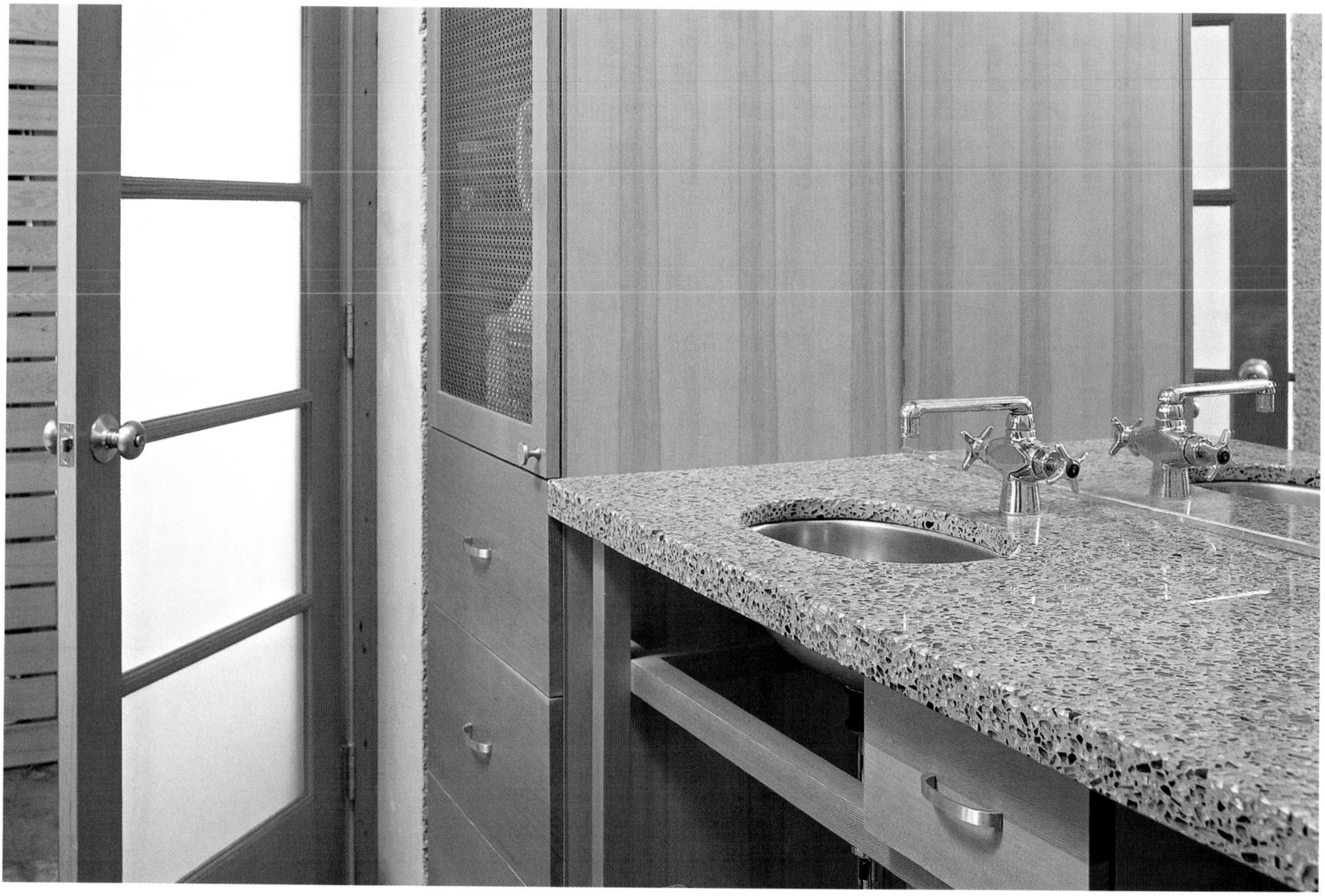

Countertop Materials

LAMINATE
$

- Attractive, hard-wearing surface available in hundreds of colors and patterns.
- Low in cost.
- Nonstaining and impervious to water.
- Works best with a drop-in sink.
- Sharp objects can scratch surface.
- Water leaks will damage substrate.

WOOD
$–$$

- Warm hues and figure of natural wood makes an earthy contrast to man-made materials.
- Can be paired with many sink types.
- Many varieties of wood can be used.
- Should be finished carefully and refinished when the surface shows signs of wear.

SOLID SURFACE
$$

- Manmade material composed of resin and a mineral filler.
- Available in a variety of colors and patterns.
- Easy to clean, nonstaining, and can be repaired.
- Can be joined with a solid-surface sink to create a seamless counter installation that won't collect grime.

NATURAL STONE
$$–$$$

- Many colors and textures are available.
- Most stone is extremely durable, but it can stain if not sealed.
- Variety of edge profiles are available.
- Needs very little maintenance.

CONCRETE
$$

- Inherently versatile.
- Can be cast in any shape and dyed to any color.
- Will stain unless sealed.
- Because of weight, should be ordered through local fabricator.

TILE
$–$$

- Many colors, sizes, and shapes are readily available.
- Wide range in prices.
- Tremendous design flexibility.
- Ceramic tile is impervious to water and very durable.
- Hard and unforgiving surface.
- Damaged tile can be replaced (set aside a few extra tiles for this purpose during installation).
- Grout lines will need sealing.

STONE COMPOSITES
$$

- Manmade material combining quartz with a small amount of resin binder.
- More stain resistant than natural stone.
- Dozens of colors are available.
- Extremely durable.

CONCRETE

STONE COMPOSITES

SOLID SURFACE

LAMINATE

left · Natural stone is a relatively expensive but durable choice for bathroom counters. Some types of stone are more porous than others, but when sealed properly stone is a low-maintenance surface.

below · Tile is a long-wearing countertop material that can be blended with other features in the room. Tile with color variation hides dirt and water spots well.

One important consideration in choosing a counter-top material is making sure it's compatible with the sink you have or are planning to get. For example, if you're planning for a solid-surface counter, consider an undermount of the same material. If you're planning a tile counter, look for a tile-edge sink, a type that's specifically designed for a flush installation in tile.

It's easy to spend a lot of money on countertops, and in some cases a top-of-the-line material might be worth it. If you're planning an overhaul of a first-floor powder room that will be frequently used by guests, you might want to choose a material that makes a big impact, like granite or marble, even if it's pricey. After all, you're not going to need very much of it. In the family bathroom upstairs, where you may have a lot more counter space and where the material will be exposed to more constant use, it's probably more sensible to go with a less expensive option, like plastic laminate.

above • Self-rimming sinks work with any type of countertop material, from stone to laminate.

above • Countertops don't have to be on one level. This two-tiered design was planned specifically for the higher cabinetry on the side, with the countertop edge blending with the edge of the backsplash.

left • A long stretch of countertop broken only by a drop-in sink offers plenty of room for toiletries.

facing page • Countertop and sink are one in this contemporary design. The warmth of the wood construction is an effective counterbalance to other materials used in the room.

Faucets

There is tremendous diversity in bathroom faucets, not only in architectural styles but also in the materials used to manufacture them and in the internal parts that are the key to trouble-free performance. When you begin looking into what kind of faucet you want, you'll probably get two pieces of advice worth heeding: Don't buy a cheap faucet, and buy your sink and faucet together so you know the two will be compatible.

Given the wide range of choices, faucets can still be divided into several broad categories—centerset, widespread, mini-widespread, and wall-mount—that are available in a number of finishes:

- Centerset faucets are one- or two-handled styles where the valves and spout are located on a shared base. One-handled models are easiest to adjust because a single lever controls both the hot and cold water lines; two-handled models have to be adjusted separately.

- Widespread faucets have a spout and two valves, all mounted separately, from 8 in. to 20 in. apart. They're typically more expensive than centerset units.

- Mini-widespread faucets are similar to widespread except that the center-to-center distance between valves is 4 in.

- Wall mounts go with above-counter sinks and often have longer-than-normal spouts to reach the basin.

top• This ornate faucet set has a formal character in keeping with the intricately detailed backsplash.

right• This classic two-handled design with a gracefully curved water spout is simple and won't lose its appeal over time.

Inside a Faucet

Faucets contain important working parts that control the flow of water. There are several types, but the one to avoid is the old-fashioned compression valve that relies on a rubber washer at the bottom of the valve stem—it's guaranteed to wear out. Better to look for a cartridge system, reliable and easy to repair, or a ceramic disc valve in which two very hard ceramic discs rotate against each other to control water flow. They often carry a lifetime guarantee.

above · This deck-mounted faucet looks something like an old-fashioned hand pump, underscoring the sink's design roots as a preplumbing washbasin.

left · Wall-mounted faucets keep the countertop uncluttered, but they require an extra level of planning with the plumber. Here, the faucet blends with the wall, allowing the tilework to take center stage.

More Faucet Options

Faucets can seem like an afterthought in a bathroom—functional but a little bland. Look a little harder and you may find a model that can become an active part of the décor. A faucet with an elaborate design, an unusual finish, or even a bit of homespun inventiveness may be a more successful match to the room than a purely traditional style.

1. This imaginative but low-tech faucet is made from a pair of simple valves and some copper pipe, a perfect complement to the informal character of the room. 2. Wall-mounted faucets are simple and out of the way. 3. The design of this mini-widespread with a curving spout works well in this contemporary bathroom.

4. Although chrome is a common material for bathroom faucets, they also are available in several other metals that are visually warmer. 5. Centerset faucets have one or two handles on a shared base. 6. Some faucets are meant to be seen, like this somewhat elaborate set that mimics the serpentine shape of the door panels. 7. A one-handled faucet is easy to operate, and this sweeping water spout is well suited to the above-counter sink. 8. Classic designs like this mini-widespread offer traditional appeal.

Toilets

Consumers have a good deal of choice when it comes to picking a new toilet. There are one- and two-piece designs, toilets with pop-off seats to aid cleaning, toilets whose water tanks are hidden inside wall cavities, and toilets that can pump waste uphill.

A conventional toilet comes in two pieces—the bowl and the tank—that are bolted together by the plumber during installation. Two-piece toilets are harder to clean than one-piece types because the seam between tank and bowl collects debris. More expensive one-piece designs have a lower, more contemporary profile, and because they are made from a single piece of china there is no visible line between tank and bowl and they are easier to keep clean. One type doesn't necessarily work any more efficiently than the other, but expect to pay a premium for the one-piece design.

above • Traditional two-piece toilets have a bowl and a tank. The tapered shape and detailing in this tank give it classic good looks.

right • One-piece toilet designs have a lower profile than two-piece models, and their seamless construction makes them easier to clean.

Toilet Wars

They may not look it, but residential toilets are very carefully designed and the object of intense competition among plumbing-supply manufacturers. By redesigning key components and manufacturing parts with greater precision, suppliers have found ways to make 1.6-gallon toilets work as well as or better than older models that use more than twice as much water.

Water usage really makes a difference. Some newer designs use even less water—1.4 gallons. That may not sound like much of a difference, but it adds up to 2,000 gallons per year for a family of four. For all the engineering changes, most toilets are still made from vitreous china, a durable and nonporous material that's inhospitable to bacteria.

above · Toilets don't have to be white or off-white. Colors can complement even very eclectic bathroom designs.

left · Basic two-piece toilets in off-white are relatively inexpensive. Improved water-conservation technology has made even economy toilets very efficient.

Bowls come in round and elongated shapes. Men may find the elongated shape more comfortable, and there also is a compact elongated bowl for bathrooms where space is limited. When it comes to seat height, the standard is 14½ in., but there also are models that meet the requirement spelled out in the Americans with Disabilities Act (ADA) of 16½ in. These toilets are now sold as "right height" or "comfort height" fixtures to broaden their appeal to consumers who will find them easier to use even if they aren't in a wheelchair.

As with other fixtures, prices of toilets vary considerably. Even with all the design choices available, the most important feature is still the toilet's ability to clear waste efficiently.

Bidets

Bidets have long been common in Europe, where daily bathing is not necessarily the norm. In the United States, where daily showers are routine for many people, this plumbing fixture has been slow to catch on. Even so, they offer obvious hygienic benefits and also can be helpful for some medical conditions. They're available as freestanding plumbing fixtures or as special toilet seats.

Toilets

Standard toilets all work on the same principle: gravity. Water is stored in a tank mounted above the bowl and released when a handle is turned or pressed. Gravity does the rest. But there also are a number of other designs.

DUAL FLUSH

- Uses a full 1.6-gallon flush for solid waste and a lesser amount for liquid waste.
- Smaller water spout than conventional U.S. design, and flow of water doesn't keep bowls as clean.
- Somewhat noisier than standard designs.
- Fewer models to choose from.

MACERATING

- Chops up waste and pumps it under pressure through a ³/₄-in. line.
- Can be installed below grade and pump effluent as much as 12 ft. vertically and 150 ft. horizontally.
- Doesn't need below-the-floor plumbing.
- Wall-mounted models are available with hidden macerator and water reservoir.

PRESSURE ASSIST

- Common in restaurants, gas stations, and other commercial venues where reliable flush is a must.
- Borrows water pressure from supply lines to help power flush or uses small electric motor.
- More expensive and noisier than a conventional toilet.
- More difficult to repair than standard designs.

left · Toilets are available in several bowl shapes, including this round design.

facing page · Manufacturers now offer suites of plumbing fixtures that make it easier to harmonize the look of a room.

TUBS AND

For many of us, bathing or showering is part of our workday routine.

For others, soaking in a hot tub or standing under jets of steaming water

SHOWERS

is a way to relax and escape. No matter how you like your water,

options abound in tub and shower design and amenities

Soaking Options

Dealing with bathtubs during a renovation can be a challenge, mainly because they are often large or heavy (or both) and difficult to maneuver down halls and through doorways. Very large tubs may be a strain on plumbing, wiring, and framing, too. But don't let that scare you off. Today there are a variety of materials used to construct tubs that make them lighter weight than ever before (and thus less costly as well). And bathtub design no longer takes a back-seat to practicality. Although millions of American bathrooms have standard-issue tubs—60 in. long and about 30 in. wide tucked into a three-walled alcove—new shapes and sizes make it possible to design a very different bathroom.

top • A wood apron and deck is one way of dressing up a conventional bathtub and creating a convenient place to park plants at the same time.

right • A large jetted tub plus an ample tub deck for towels and toiletries is a good way of getting a spa-like experience at home.

facing page • Where privacy isn't a pressing issue, position the tub to take advantage of the dramatic views.

WHIRLPOOL TUBS

First developed about 40 years ago, whirlpool tubs—those with jets that circulate water while you're soaking—are now commonplace. No matter what the size (one person or two), all whirlpool tubs rely on the same basic technology, but what is no longer so basic are the options for how to incorporate a jetted tub into a bathroom.

Whirlpool tubs come in two basic types: apron-front tubs that are designed for an alcove, and drop-in designs that are built into a deck surrounding the tub. Large whirlpools are usually made from acrylic. Smaller sizes can be acrylic or cast iron. All jetted tubs can be customized to suit individual tastes by varying the number and location of jets

right • If there's enough room, a large tub can be housed in a raised platform that includes a broad step, making it easy to get in and out of the water.

bottom right • Dual faucets are a pullout to make rinsing easier—put water just where it's wanted.

facing page • A large whirlpool tub often becomes the focal point of the bathroom, its prominence here emphasized by the circular window and the pitched ceiling above.

A tiled bench adjacent to this tub surround offers a convenient place to sit while the tub is filling. Visually, the bench ties the room together.

Reviving Old Tubs

Rather than replace an old bathtub, you can repair a stained or damaged tub with a new acrylic liner and tub surround or apply a new finish to the tub surface.

Relining a tub isn't inexpensive, but it's faster and neater than tearing one out. Once a technician has made measurements and placed the order, it usually takes a week or two for a new liner and surround to arrive. Installation takes about a day.

Old fixtures also can be refinished. The process involves etching the interior of the tub with a solution of hydrofluoric acid, filling in chips with polyester resin, and then applying a primer and acrylic urethane topcoat. The whole repair should take a half-day. Cast iron, acrylic, fiberglass gelcoat, and cultured marble fixtures all can be repaired. Keep in mind, though, that the finish on a repaired cast iron tub won't last nearly as long as the original.

THE ESSENTIALS

Bathtubs

Tubs come in all kinds of shapes, sizes, and price ranges. What the tub is made from has a lot to do with how it looks, how long it will last, and how much maintenance it will need to look its best.

FIBERGLASS/GELCOAT
$

- Made by spraying a mold with a thin layer of polyester resin called gelcoat and then adding layers of fiberglass for strength.
- Common material in combination tub/shower units.
- Inexpensive but not as durable as other options.
- Can be damaged by abrasive cleaners; follow manufacturer's recommendations.

PORCELAIN OVER STEEL
$

- Made by coating a shell of steel with a layer of heat-fused porcelain enamel.
- Similar to a porcelain enamel cast iron tub, only not as durable.
- Lighter than cast iron.
- Surface is stain and abrasion resistant and easy to clean, but steel will rust if surface is chipped.

ACRYLIC
$$

- Lightweight plastic fixtures made from a sheet of acrylic in a vacuum mold and reinforced with fiberglass.
- Color goes all the way through the material so minor scratches don't show.
- More durable than fiberglass, but follow manufacturer's recommendations on cleaners.

CULTURED MARBLE
$$

- Manufactured by mixing marble dust with polyester resin and pigments to mimic the look of stone.
- Shower surrounds and sinks can be made at the same time to create a suite of bathroom fixtures in custom colors.
- Gelcoat surface is not porous and resists stains, but it can be damaged by abrasive cleaners.

PORCELAIN ENAMEL OVER CAST IRON
$$–$$$

- Heavy, long wearing, easy to keep clean, and stain resistant.
- More durable than most other tubs.
- Manufacturing process in which porcelain enamel is bonded to a very hot iron core ensures a deep, lustrous finish.
- Retains heat and deadens sound.

COPPER AND BRONZE
$$$

- Copper and bronze tubs retain heat like cast iron.
- Virtually indestructible.
- Keeping these metals glistening requires some elbow grease.

A large tub with a hand shower can take the place of a conventional shower stall. Center-mounted faucets allow bathers to rest against either end of the tub.

There are, however, a couple of things to keep in mind before trying to squeeze a large whirlpool into your bathroom. They take up a lot of floor space, may get used less frequently than you think initially, and usually require a dedicated electrical circuit to power pumps and heaters. In addition, whirlpools need regular maintenance to prevent the growth of bacteria in internal water lines.

In less-extensive remodeling projects, restoring a tub or shower may be an attractive option, either because a replacement fixture costs too much or will take too long to install. A chipped porcelain tub can be refinished by a specialty contractor and old tubs also can be covered with a new acrylic shell.

top • This room is all about the bathing experience: The size of the tub and its surround, its central location beneath a raised ceiling, and an encircling band of windows all make that obvious.

left • A large tub doesn't have to dominate the room. Here, the light colors of the tub, floor, and walls minimize size, and wood in the ceiling, around windows, and in the vanity help give those features more vitality.

facing page • Simple and inviting, this large tub is surrounded by carefully chosen materials that form a welcoming enclosure. A simple ladder makes an effective towel rack.

AIR-JET TUBS

Unlike whirlpool tubs that use jets of air and water, these tubs rely on jets of air bubbles to massage and relax. Some air-jet tubs have as many as 70 nozzles built into the walls and floor of the tub to dispense streams of warm air bubbles. One advantage to this type of fixture is that they're not as susceptible as whirlpool tubs to bacterial growth because water is not circulated through the plumbing. Some models automatically purge air lines after the tub is drained to reduce maintenance. One- and two-person models are available, as well as tubs that have both air jets and whirlpool nozzles and even built-in lights.

New Tub Punch List

Interested in replacing your 5-ft. bathtub with a larger whirlpool? Consider these factors:

- **Weight.** A big tub can hold a couple hundred gallons of water and weigh a ton. Floor framing may need reinforcement.
- **Electrical service.** Large whirlpools need dedicated 220-volt circuits to power pumps and auxiliary heaters.
- **Water supply.** Your water heater should have at least three-quarters the capacity of the tub. Don't try to run a 120-gallon tub with an 80-gallon water heater.
- **Budget.** A bathtub is only one part of a remodeling project. Make sure this one fixture does not use a disproportionate share of what you have to spend.

DETAILS THAT WORK

Foot Spa

Tub options include this dedicated foot spa from MTI Whirlpools®. It's about 2 ft. square and 12 in. deep and comes equipped with four directional jets. It's just the ticket if you've spent the day on your feet.

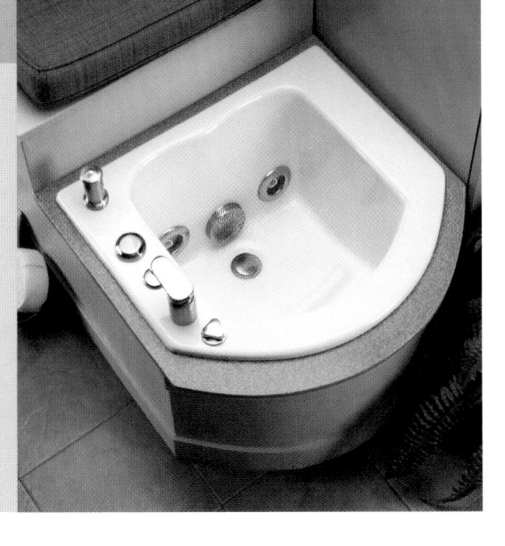

below • This tub surrounds mimics the architectural details in the rest of the room, tying all elements of the space together. The use of white allows the view outside to become the focal point.

facing page • Roll-up woven window shades bring natural texture into this room, which is complemented by other textures, including the tiled tub surround and countertop and wicker storage bin. The exposed beams in the roof give the tub area a haven-like feel.

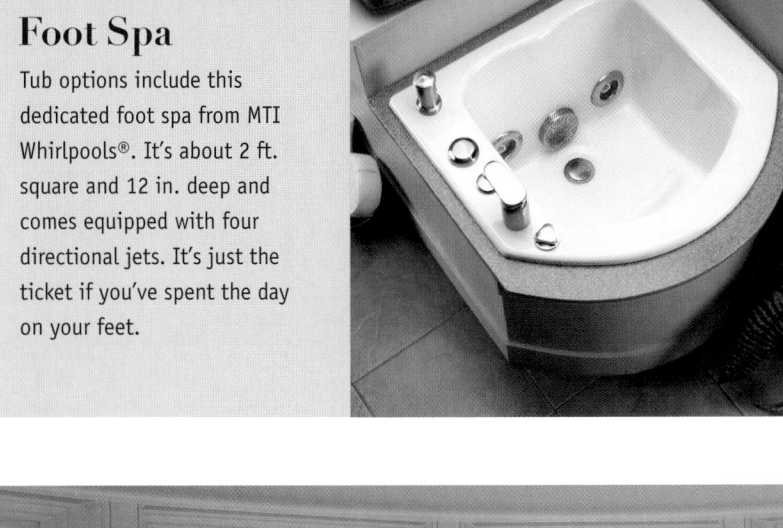

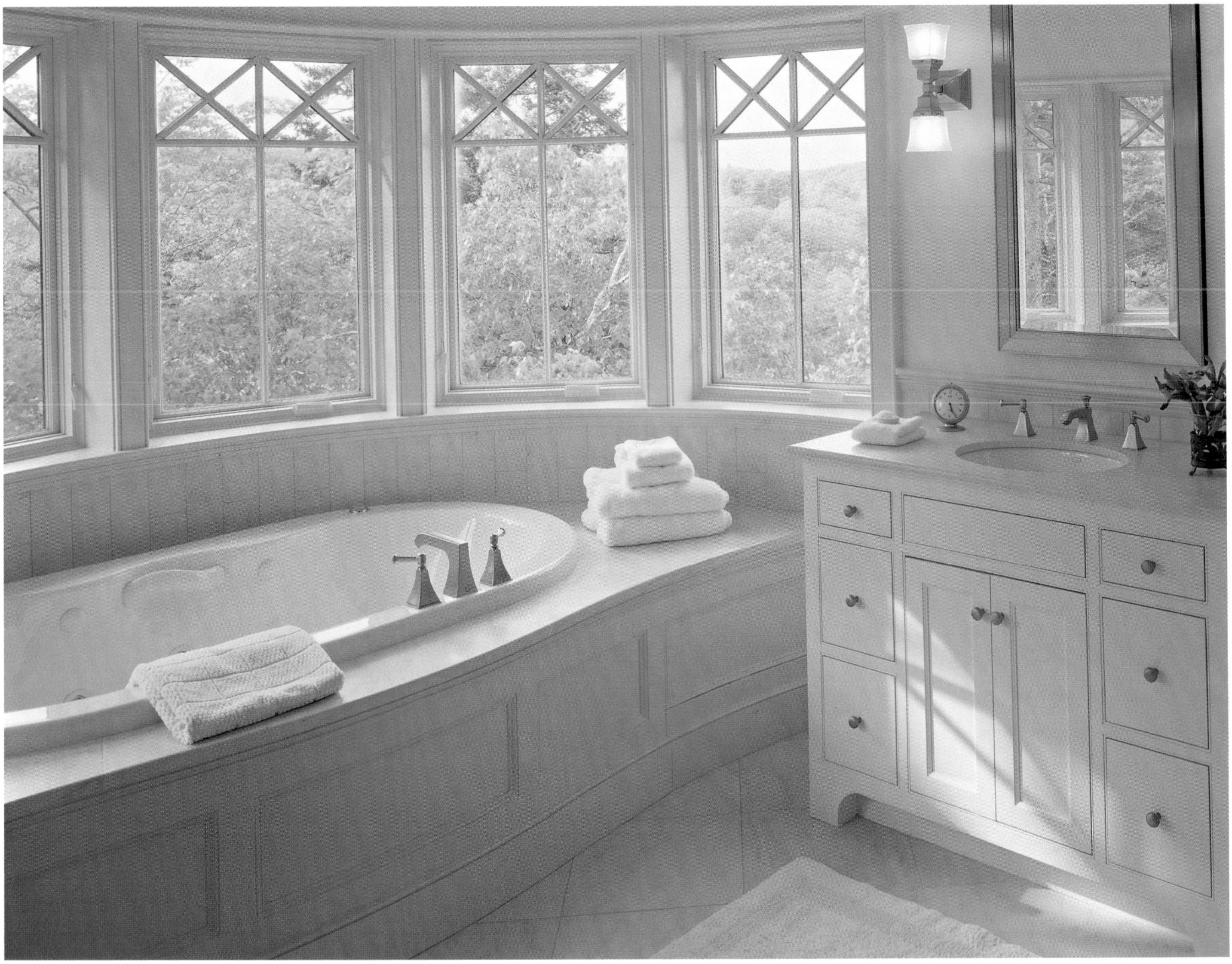

JAPANESE-STYLE TUBS

Japanese bathing rituals are somewhat different than ours. The operative word here is ritual—a leisurely, chin-deep soak in a tub of scalding hot water at day's end and only after you've washed thoroughly in another part of the bathroom. The vehicle for this venerated routine is a bathtub that can be twice as deep as the American standard. Called *ofuros* in Japan, they were traditionally built from wood and had square sides, but now are widely available in acrylic plastic on the Internet as well as from conventional retailers in America. They can be purchased either as free-standing or drop-in tubs and even as whirlpool models. Small ones don't take up very much floor space, making them candidates for remodels of relatively small bathrooms.

top right • In an interesting mix of styles and materials, the wood floor, simple side chair, and Shaker-feeling towel pegs provide warmth to the expanse of light-colored marble and curtainless window.

above • Deep soaking tubs allow a bather a chin-deep soak at the end of a long day. They come in a variety of styles.

right • This glass shower enclosure makes the bathroom feel more spacious and prevent the tub area from feeling closed in.

facing page • The beautiful wood tub surround and wall partition provide warmth and coziness to this bathing area even though the bathroom is quite large.

Building a Custom Tub

A second-floor addition with a new bathroom gave the contractor and architect an opportunity to create this custom soaking tub and open-style shower.

The client wanted a deep soaking tub that two people could use. This one is about 36 in. deep and includes a shallow seat whose height was set by experimenting with stacks of books until the sitting position was comfortable. In the Japanese tradition, bathers can wash in an adjacent shower before plunging into the tub.

On the opposite side of the bathroom, slate is used on the vanity countertop and on the short wall separating the toilet from the rest of the room. That helps to unify the room. Woodwork, however, is light in color, an effective counterbalance to the visual weight of the stone.

top right • The height of a low bench inside this slate-lined soaking tub was determined after experimenting with stacks of books. The natural veining in the slate ties the colors of the bathroom together.

right • Gray-black slate and light-color wood tones are complemented by simple hardware and fixtures.

left · Operable windows are a great addition to any bathroom. Due to its size, this one lets in a lot of light in addition to an abundance of air.

Slipper Tubs

Old fashioned slipper tubs are similar in appearance to more conventional claw-foots except that one end sweeps up to form a comfortable back rest for lounging or reading. Combined with elaborately detailed feet and chrome or brass supply and drain lines, these tubs have a distinctly period look. Slipper tubs are also available as double-enders so the bather can relax against either end of the tub.

Tub Styles

Once limited to just a few sizes, colors, and styles, bathtubs are now available in enough variety to suit any bathroom and remodeling budget. In smaller spaces a standard 5-ft. rectangular tub or a refurbished claw-foot may still be the most practical choice. But when there's more room to spare, and a more generous construction budget, a jetted tub big enough for two, a deep Japanese-style tub, or a tub made for a cozy corner may be just the ticket. Whatever your preference, you should be able to find a tub to match.

1. This large soaking tub enjoys a commanding view of an outdoor space. Making a connection with the outside makes the room seem larger and more spacious.
2. A large tub made to fit in a corner offers more options for laying out a comfortable bathroom.

3. A claw-foot tub is a good choice for a period bathroom. The outside of this tub has been painted to blend with the room's decor. **4.** Accessorize your tub—and bathing experience—with readily available caddies and organizers. **5.** A raised tub topped by a series of tall windows becomes the central feature of this bathroom, and provides great views to the outside.

Showers

New showers are key to making bathrooms less utilitarian and more spa-like. Conventional shower stalls and shower/tub combinations—equipped with a single showerhead—will probably never go out of style. They're practical and inexpensive. But when enlarging or upgrading a master bath you have an opportunity to turn it into something more than a place for a quick scrub. High-output shower panels, recirculating pumps, custom multihead installations, hand-held spray heads, and steam generators all are options when you're rethinking the basic shower.

Large, well-equipped showers share similarities with whirlpools and soaking tubs. Both are designed to elevate bathing from a routine chore to what many now think of as an "experience." In the process both can consume a lot of hot water. But unlike a tub, a shower can be used almost as soon as it's turned on. There's no waiting for all that hot water to be drawn, making a shower upgrade an appealing idea for someone who doesn't have time for a leisurely soak.

top left • A generous bench and a window make this shower a place for more than just a quick cleaning. The showerhead encourages enjoyment.

top right • An oversize shower becomes the visual focal point for this bathroom thanks to the dramatic coloring of its marble walls and floor.

right • A half-wall separating the shower from the rest of the bathroom makes the room much brighter than a full shower enclosure would allow. Windows inside the shower bring in extra light.

facing page • The placement of the glass-walled shower in the center of this bathroom is unusual, but the transparent walls allow natural light to bathe the entire room.

Locating the shower and tub next to each other under a sloping ceiling was the best way to make use of the available space. In the shower, glass block lets light in but ensures privacy.

It's easy to think of a shower as nothing more than a box with a door or curtain separating it from the rest of the room. Many showers are exactly that. There isn't much flexibility with an acrylic or fiberglass/gelcoat shower module, for example, or a cast iron tub built into a standard 5-ft. alcove. But designers have found more interesting ways to integrate showers into an overall bathroom design, using glass block, sheets of glass, half-walls, and even an absence of walls to define a space set aside for showering.

Working with tile, stone, or a solid-surface material such as Corian®, a shower installer can create virtually any shape or configuration to fit your available space: showers with glass-block walls, showers with curvaceous walls but no doors, all-glass showers that are flooded with natural light, showers with their own windows or skylights. Choices in tile and stone also means you can get virtually any look you want, from clean and spare to flamboyant.

top • Imaginative tilework is on display due to the glass shower walls. Tile set diagonally on the lower shower walls mimics the pattern on the floor.

far left • A band of dark accent tile wraps around the inside of this shower and gives the walls some definition. A shower bench is perfect for holding soap and shampoo.

left • This corner shower is illuminated by a long skylight. Shower walls of glass reflect the light, making the most of it.

Same Room, More Space

This remodeled bathroom is a good example of the less-is-more theory. The design gives up a standard-size bathtub that had been located along one wall and replaces it with a generous vanity and sink. Gone are the existing pedestal sink and radiator—as well as outdated floor and wall tile in shades of pink and green.

The result is a more spacious bathroom with an appealing color scheme, modern fixtures, and a big, welcoming shower. What hasn't changed is the location of the toilet and the shower drain, a time and money saver. By working with the existing footprint and concentrating on essential fixtures—the shower and the vanity—the designer has transformed the room without disrupting the house.

bottom · This redesigned bathroom incorporates a vanity where a standard-size bathtub had been, creating more room for storage and an attractive area for grooming.

bottom right · Removing a radiator made this room more spacious and cleared the way for a new tiled shower.

BEFORE

Glass is an ideal material for shower doors and walls because it transmits light, preventing the shower from feeling like a cave and allowing the overall room to look more open and spacious. Some door and wall assemblies have relatively thick frames that support glass panels. Doors, however, can be hinged directly to the wall without a frame, and when used in tandem with unframed glass panels, the effect on the room is entirely different.

When considering a glass door, though, remember that whatever is on the other side—from colorful mosaic tiles and beautiful outdoor views to toiletries and soapscum that needs cleaning—will be on display for all to see.

left · **The green tile is a powerful design element in this bathroom, thanks to the sheet of glass separating the tub from the rest of the bathroom.**

EASY-ACCESS SHOWERS

A shower also can be designed with only a partial wall and no door at all to separate it from the rest of the bathroom. Keeping the tops of shower walls below ceiling height helps to integrate the shower with the rest of the room. In these installations, showerheads are directed away from the door so splashing is minimal, and a raised curb at the entry keeps water from escaping into the bathroom.

To carry the idea one step further, curbless showers allow floors to flow seamlessly all the way through the room with no impediments that would hinder a wheelchair. This is a fundamental premise of what's called "universal design," but it's also an interesting feature in a household where wheelchair access isn't an issue. There's nothing for the foot, or the eye, to trip over. A curbless shower, however, does require some careful planning.

A generously sized shower plus careful placement of the showerhead make it possible to skip the shower door. Stepped walls help the shower seem more like a part of the room.

The mass of this glass-block shower enclosure is lessened by stepped-down corners. Glass block makes an opaque wall but still allows plenty of light inside the shower enclosure.

top • A large shower like this one can accommodate more than one person at a time—each with his or her own showerhead.

above • Careful design makes it possible to eliminate the shower door completely. The entrance to this shower is marked by a massive column.

Not only is the design of showers reaching new heights, but so are shower fixtures. They now come with varying numbers of showerheads and body jets. Some plumbers can also create a completely custom multihead shower with the style and location of different heads to suit your preferences.

Anti-scald valves, required by code in most renovated and new baths, offer protection against sudden changes in pressure between hot and cold water supplies. A good valve, though expensive, is cheap insurance against scalds or injuries.

above • Glass shower walls allow light from a window in the shower to reach into the rest of the bathroom.

right • Exposed timbers in the roof became an expressive part of the shower enclosure, an effect enhanced by glass shower walls.

Multihead Showers

Shower towers and jetted panels can make your shower seem like a water park. Designs originated in Europe, where invasive changes to in-wall plumbing are often difficult due to the way houses are built. Some of these fixtures are attached to the shower wall at only two points and then connected to hot and cold water lines, making them good candidates for a remodel in which an existing shower is still sound.

Panels with a variety of water outlets are available. One model, for example, has seven, including two adjustable showerheads, four body sprays, and a hand-held shower. Overhead showers can be moved up and down on telescoping posts. Body sprays also are adjustable. Don't like the intensity of the spray? That's something else that can be altered to suit your mood.

But performance like that gobbles up a lot of water. Federal regulations limit the output of showerheads to 2.5 gallons per minute, but because these shower towers have multiple heads the consumption of water can be far greater and may need oversize supply lines. In addition, you may need a dedicated hot-water heater.

top • You might feel like you're going through a car wash when your shower features multiple showerheads and body sprays.

far left • This panel incorporates ten jets of water. A pump recirculates the water, so it's not as wasteful as it appears at first glance.

left • Showers can feature a unit with multiple showerheads and body jets that can be adjusted to suit individual preferences.

Showerhead Upgrades

There are a number of simple upgrades that can make an existing shower more functional and more attractive without breaking the bank. One of them is replacing that anemic showerhead with one that makes taking a shower more like standing in a warm summer rain. Another step up is adding a hand-held shower, either as a replacement for a standard showerhead or as a complement to one.

1. This supplementary showerhead can be adjusted in height or removed and used as a hand-held shower. 2. This high-end shower valve and diverter has a charming Old World feel. 3. A swiveling showerhead can be adjusted to deliver a vigorous massage or a soft spray.

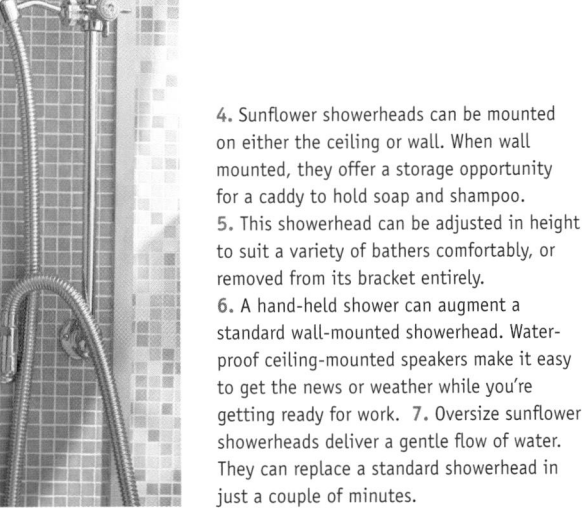

4. Sunflower showerheads can be mounted on either the ceiling or wall. When wall mounted, they offer a storage opportunity for a caddy to hold soap and shampoo.
5. This showerhead can be adjusted in height to suit a variety of bathers comfortably, or removed from its bracket entirely.
6. A hand-held shower can augment a standard wall-mounted showerhead. Waterproof ceiling-mounted speakers make it easy to get the news or weather while you're getting ready for work. 7. Oversize sunflower showerheads deliver a gentle flow of water. They can replace a standard showerhead in just a couple of minutes.

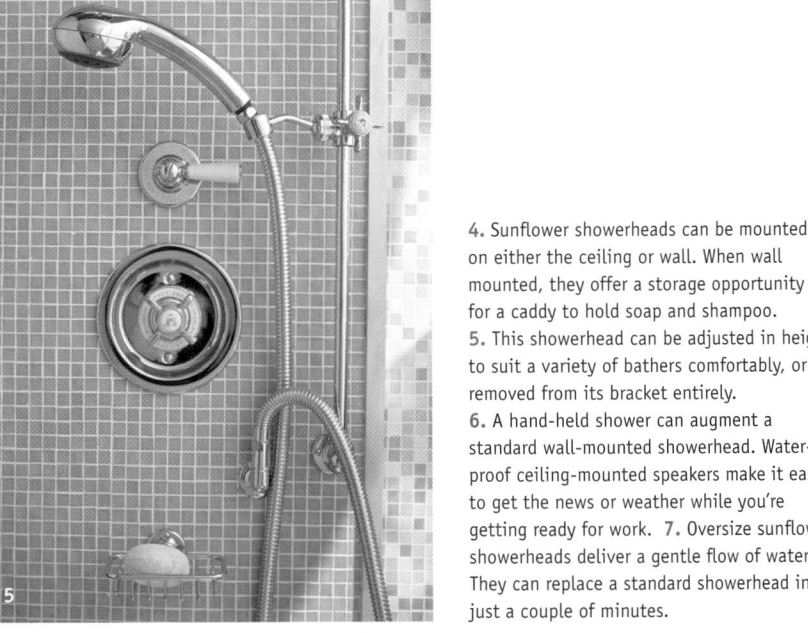

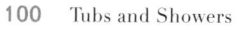

Offbeat Shower

Ordinary ½-in. copper pipe becomes a graceful shower supply in this renovated bathroom. This unusual supply seems to merge with the shower curtain support that encircles the claw-foot tub. A wall-hung stainless steel sink reinforces the room's eclectic sensibility and contributes to an overall relaxed feeling.

Finally, sprucing up a shower may involve nothing more difficult than choosing a new shower curtain to add a splash of color or a vibrant pattern to an otherwise plain room. Even changing the curtain rod and hardware can add an inexpensive and instant update. Although glass shower doors are often the norm, fabric offers an entirely different kind of design option at much lower cost. Look for shower curtains that have coordinating window treatments to tie the room together.

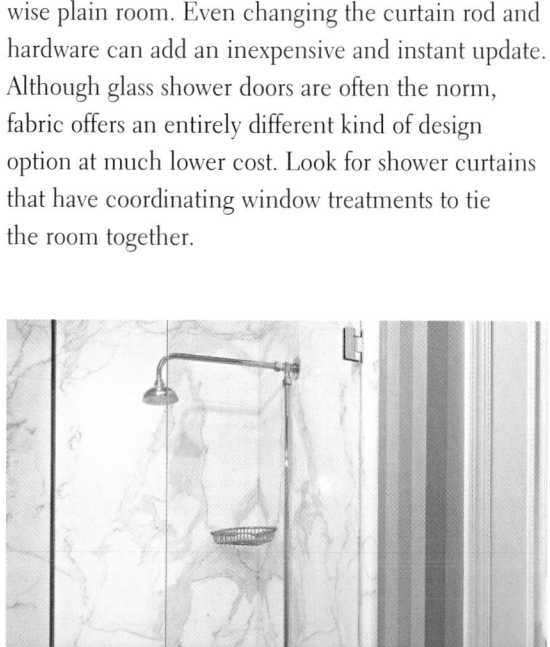

above · The warm tones of the showerhead and arm complement the marble interior of this shower.

left · Adding a patterned fabric shower curtain is a quick way to spruce up a bathroom—and it's fairly inexpensive to replace when styles or tastes change.

facing page · A small amount of color can pack a lot of punch, as it does in this mostly off-white bathroom.

New Bath in a Foursquare

Updating this bathroom in a 1910 American foursquare solved a variety of functional and aesthetic problems. In the original layout, the toilet was the first thing you'd encounter as you opened the door, whereas the sink was tucked in a far corner beyond the tub. A closet managed to camouflage part of a stairwell, but it took up valuable floor space while offering little in the way of storage. The bathroom's medicine cabinet was inoperable.

In the remodeled space, the sink and toilet have been swapped to make the room less congested. A large console sink with ample room for toiletries takes the place of the wall-mounted medicine cabinet. A custom-built cabinet with more storage replaces the closet, and a heater hidden beneath the bench at the far end of the shower allows the radiator to disappear. Instead of a standard bathtub, the homeowners now enjoy a large shower.

The end result is a bathroom that's more efficient, brighter, and more comfortable. Careful selection of materials helps. The homeowners chose classic white subway tile capped by a band of wine-red accent tiles and then a chair rail. Richly patterned wallpaper complements the pale green color of the slate floor, and the large glass-walled shower helps to make the room seem more spacious.

BEFORE

Relocating the toilet and sink, reversing the door swing, and replacing the tub with a glass-walled shower were among the important improvements in this remodeled bathroom that originally dates from the early 1900s.

BEFORE

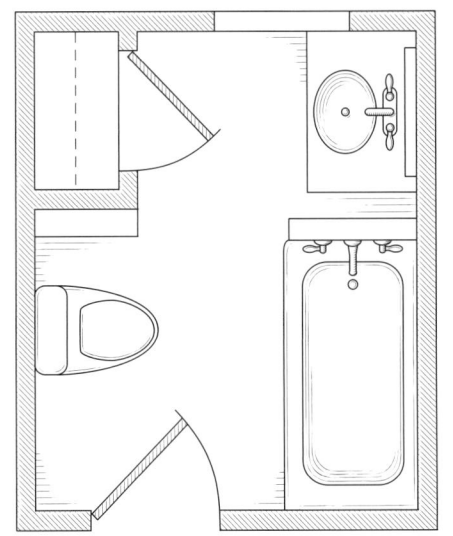

AFTER

Built-in cabinet hides the stairwell ceiling

The new plan makes better use of the space by swapping fixtures and changing the door swing.

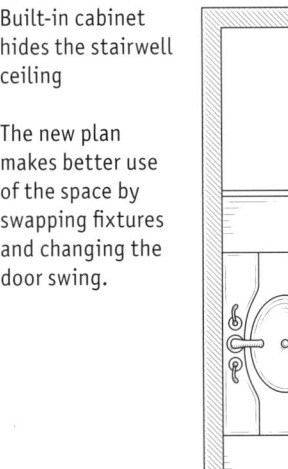

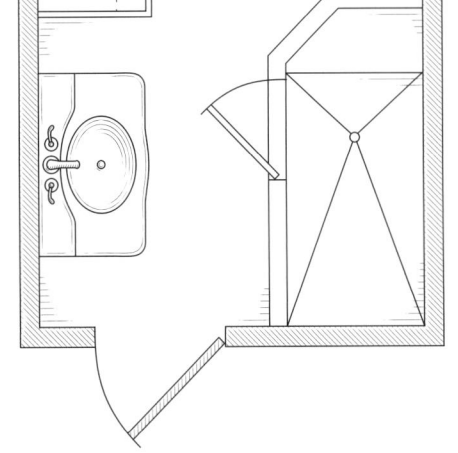

above · A steam radiator in the original bathroom made the room seem cramped. Installing a heater beneath the shower bench allowed the radiator to be removed.

left · In the remodeled bathroom, the sink is moved toward the front of the room, with the toilet taking its place in the corner. A glass-walled shower replaces the tub, and a new custom cabinet in the corner takes the place of an inefficient closet.

FLOORS,

Although tough-as-nails materials are a must for the longevity of this

hard-working room, don't forget that color, texture, and patterns have

a big impact on what a bathroom ultimately looks like.

WALLS, AND

Balancing practical and aesthetic considerations to get the right mix

of performance and appearance is really at the heart of making

the best surface choices in any bath.

CEILINGS

Floors, walls, and ceilings make up most of the visible surfaces in a bathroom, and the materials you choose must be able to thrive under some trying conditions. The chief threat, of course, is water—splashes from the sink and tub as well as high levels of humidity that at times make the room feel like a rain forest. Long-term damage from moisture is one of the main reasons many older bathrooms have to be remodeled in the first place.

Even if your house was built only 25 years ago, hardly a blink when you think of all the 18th-century houses that still exist, you'll find that in addition to the old standards there are now a surprising number of new building materials—better grades of vinyl flooring, ceramic tile that looks a lot like stone, and engineered wood that's more stable than solid lumber. With so many more choices, it's easy to find the appropriate material for a particular bathroom: highly water-resistant and durable surfaces in a children's bathroom and visually pleasing materials in a master bath or powder room, for instance.

top left · Tile is an unusually versatile material that can be used on floors, walls, and even ceilings. Different tile sizes and materials can be combined in the same room.

top right · A variety of historic wallpaper patterns are available, a perfect accent for a bathroom in a period home.

left · A floor doesn't have to be dull. This colorful and asymmetrical pattern is carried over from the floor to the tub surround to create a lively, contemporary look.

facing page · A floor of small hexagonal tiles is durable and attractive, and the small tiles are easy to work into out-of-square corners, typical in older houses.

Floors

Although it may seem subtle—after all, we have to look down to notice it—the floor has a lot to do with our perception of the room. Floors that reflect light make rooms brighter and create a feeling of spaciousness, whereas dark, textured floors have a heavy, rustic quality. But there are practical considerations, too, because the floor is especially vulnerable to standing water.

Today there are at least a half-dozen widely available materials in a variety of prices that are suitable for bathroom flooring. Some of them—vinyl, tile, and engineered flooring, for instance—don't necessarily require that existing flooring be removed before they can be installed, making them best for renovations that do not include a complete room overhaul. Others—some types of natural stone tile, for instance—are not so forgiving and may not be the best choice for a retrofit. Instead, they are more suitable in situations where rooms are stripped down to the framing and rebuilt.

Tile wainscoting is a practical, easy-to-clean surface that will long outlast plaster or drywall. Here it flows gracefully into a tiled floor whose intricate pattern helps it look like carpet.

Flooring

A key consideration in choosing bathroom flooring is water resistance. But it's less of an issue in a guest bath used only occasionally or a powder room intended for visitors than it is in an everyday bathroom for a family with children. Beyond their ability to stand up to water, the textures and colors inherent in different kinds of flooring also are important design tools.

STONE

LAMINATE

TILE

TILE
$–$$

- Highly durable.
- Available in an enormous range of colors, sizes, and surface textures that allow unrivaled design flexibility.
- Glazed tile is not affected by high levels of humidity or water. Grout lines can be sealed against moisture and stains.
- Can be installed over some types of existing floors, but watch out for bouncy floors in older houses—tiles may crack.
- In cold weather tile will feel cold to the feet unless some kind of radiant floor heat has been installed.
- Look for a textured surface that won't be too slippery when it gets wet.

WOOD
$–$$

- Available in solid planks and strips as well as engineered versions in a number of different species.

- Naturally beautiful color and grain markings that range from plain to flamboyant.

- Warm and comfortable underfoot.

- Like laminate flooring, prefinished wood flooring can be walked on immediately after installation.

- Will be damaged by continued exposure to water; worn finishes speed process.

- Not a completely stable material; shrinks and expands with changes in moisture levels and humidity.

STONE
$$–$$$

- Beautiful natural variety in color and texture.

- Extremely durable.

- Highly polished varieties are slippery when wet.

- Requires rigid floor framing and subfloor to prevent bounce that could crack stone.

- Marble and limestone most susceptible to cracking; slate the least.

- Requires sealing.

VINYL
$

- Lots of colors and patterns available.

- Warm and resilient underfoot.

- Inlaid versions offer tough wear layer and good durability.

- Relatively inexpensive.

- Unaffected by water, making it an ideal choice in a child's bathroom.

- Lacks the visual appeal of natural materials like stone or wood.

LAMINATE
$

- Installs easily and quickly.

- Available in a variety of patterns made to look like wood.

- Inexpensive.

- Durable top layer resists wear.

- Use only in a powder room or a bathroom where splashing water and high levels of humidity are unlikely.

WOOD

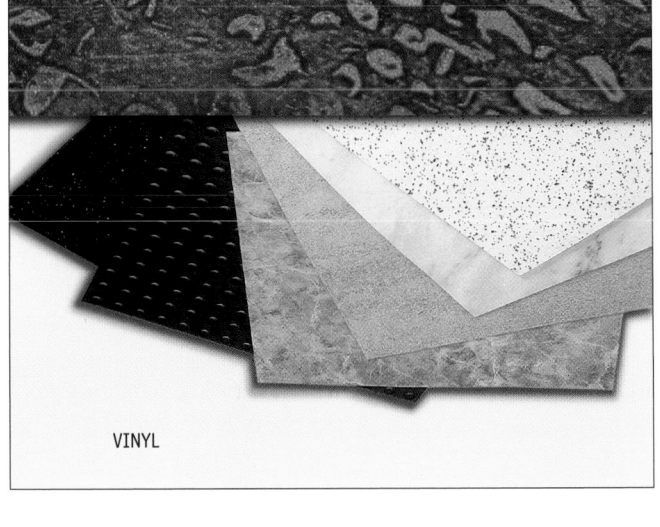

VINYL

TILE

Ceramic tile is a popular surface for bathroom floors for several good reasons: It's available in many sizes, colors, textures, and prices; it can be installed over some existing floors; it's adaptable to rooms in older houses where floors are no longer level and square; and it will last a very long time when installed properly. Moreover, tile requires very little maintenance once the grout between the tiles is sealed against staining.

Of all these attributes, tile's versatility is really at the top of the list. Tile comes in sizes from 1-in. to 24-in. rectangular, square, octagonal, and hexagonal shapes. It can be installed on the diagonal to make a small bathroom look larger, taken right up the walls to form dramatic and easy-to-clean wainscoting, or varied by shape, color, and size to create visually appealing borders and patterns. Rich effects can be had by placing fancy (and pricey) accent tiles in a field of otherwise standard floor tiles. Using larger-size and light-colored tiles in a small bathroom are two other ways of making it seem bigger than it actually is.

For bathroom floors, glazed ceramic and porcelain tiles are the best choice because of their durability and high water resistance. They can also be made to look surprisingly like stone, but at a lower cost. Unglazed pavers, such as Mexican Saltillos, have an attractive, earthy color and texture, but they're porous so they need to be sealed and periodically resealed. Unless they're cracked or broken, ceramic and porcelain tiles won't need that kind of care.

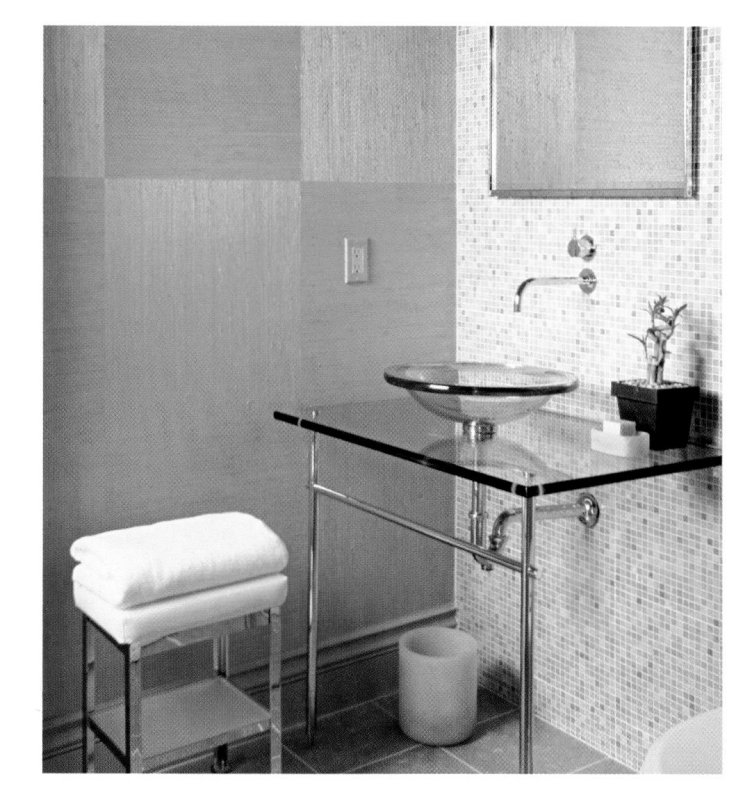

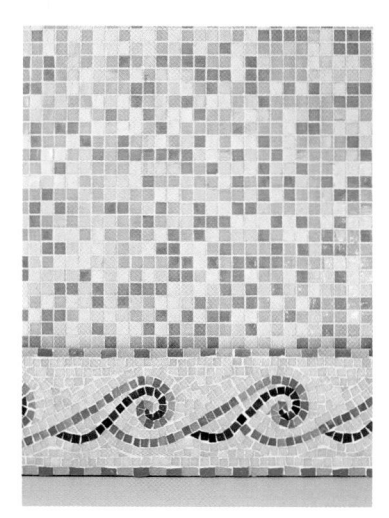

top • Two distinct yet complementary wall patterns use large and small tile in the same neutral colors. Thanks to the glass vanity, the wall of tiny tile mosaics can be appreciated without interruption from floor to ceiling.

right • Mosaics are one way of introducing patterns and colors to walls and floors. This wave theme would complement a seaside bathroom.

far right • White tile doesn't have to be dull. Small squares of blue at the corners of this diagonally laid floor complement the cool marble color around the bath and give the bathroom a crisp, contemporary feel.

With a palette of only black and white, this bathroom manages to have a lively, contemporary flavor. Clear glass shower walls don't break up the effect.

Another advantage of tile is that it can be laid over some other types of flooring. If the existing floor is vinyl that's still well bonded to the subfloor, for example, an installer can put down a new layer of tile without tearing out the old floor. Tile, however, needs a stable substrate. It can't be installed directly over a wood plank floor that shrinks and swells with seasonal changes in humidity. Unlike wood flooring, tile is not very tolerant of flexing; too much movement in a floor will lead to cracked grout joints and even cracked tiles. If the floor feels wobbly, especially in the center of the room, it may be a sign that real work must be done on the structure of the floor before tile can be set.

Traction by the Numbers

The tile industry actually has a number to describe how slippery a tile is, called the coefficient of friction (COF). It's probably enough to ask the tilesetter or builder for tile that has enough surface texture to minimize slips. If you're interested in the fine print, the industry recommends a minimum COF of 0.50 (wet and dry) to be considered slip resistant (standards are higher for bathrooms meeting provisions of the Americans with Disabilities Act).

New Tile Saves an Old Bathroom

This second-floor guest bathroom in a 1905 California Craftsman style house is a good example of how a few carefully considered changes can make a dramatic improvement in how a room looks. The existing bathroom had been renovated during the 1970s, but with a light-blocking partition at the end of the shower, a dated plywood vanity, and dreary floor tiles the room hardly put on a cheerful face for guests.

To help keep costs in check, plumbing fixtures were not moved. But bright subway tile on the walls, an appealing pattern of hexagonal floor tile, and a lowered shower partition give the room an entirely different look. A bold perimeter border on the floor, along with some artful tilesetting, helped disguise out-of-square corners. Tile contractors also used backer board and mortar to level the sloping but structurally sound floor. Swapping a new pedestal sink for the old vanity helped to make the room seem less crowded.

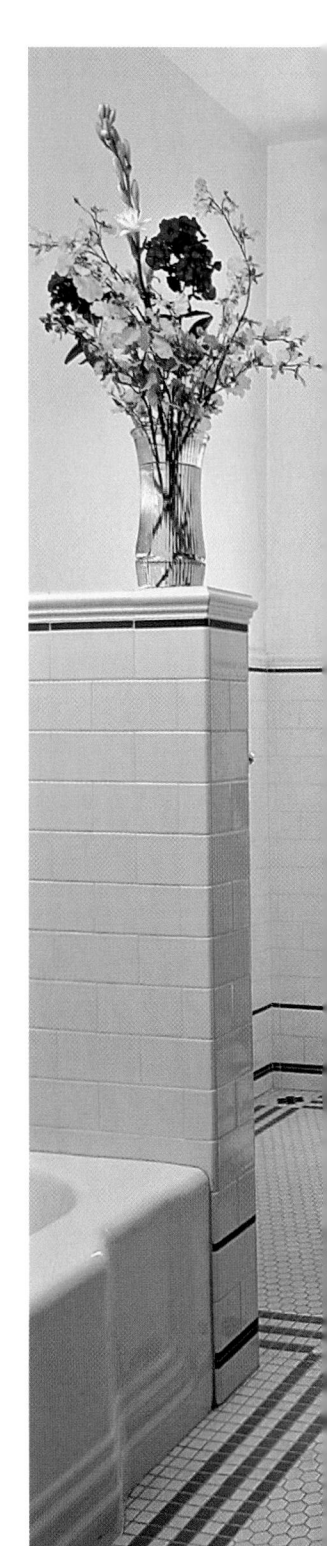

right · Tile borders at the edge of the floor and at the top and bottom of the wainscoting on the wall draw this bathroom together.

bottom right · Thanks to skillful tile installation and the material itself, it's hard to tell that this corner really isn't square.

BEFORE

If the floor is torn up during the remodel, the builder will be able to beef up the framing by adding new joists next to what's already there, or by adding additional layers of subfloor to make the floor stiffer. But these steps have the potential of adding thickness to the floor and making the transition to adjacent rooms or hallways awkward. There can also be considerable variation in tile thickness, which can complicate clearances under doors and cabinets.

It's best to look for floor tile with enough texture that it won't be too slippery when wet (avoid highly polished marble on the floor, for example). But with the proper precautions, like a decent-size floor rug, tile has many other flooring options beat. One other caution about tile: Always buy a little extra in case you need to replace damaged tile down the road. You may not be able to find the identical pattern or color again.

Tile Rug

Traditionally used in Mediterranean climates to add carpet-like patterns and colors to a room while keeping it cool, tile rugs are now a mainstay of many tile manufacturers. This is a pennywise way to use handcrafted or expensive tiles in a unique setting, adding texture and color variation to a small or large bathroom.

Multicolored tiles that pick up hues elsewhere in the room help to make a coherent décor.

STONE

Natural stone can have a powerful effect on the overall feel of a bathroom. It's a tremendously diverse material, available in many colors, thicknesses, and textures, and it can have a powerful effect on the overall feel of a bathroom. Consider, for example, the difference between a bathroom with floors and shower walls finished in a dark textured stone like slate and a bathroom dominated by a light colored, highly polished stone like marble. Stone also is a very durable material that should last as long as the house—or easily until the next remodel.

That said, stone has some quirks. Because stone is natural, color and veining can vary from individual tile to individual tile. Although this variation can add real presence to the design, it can also mean that the floor won't feel like one whole surface. With the exception of some kinds of soapstone, natural stone also should be sealed to prevent staining. Some types of stone, such as lighter shades of marble, should be periodically resealed.

From a remodeling standpoint there's one more thing to consider: Stone is even less tolerant of bouncy floors than ceramic tile, so all of the cautions that go along with remodeling a bathroom floor with ceramic tile apply doubly with stone.

top right · Tile can be made to look like another material. The mosaics bordering this floor resemble the edges of a carpet.

right · Cool stone and warm wood make an effective combination in this bathroom. Using the same material on the tub surround and walls pulls the room together.

facing page · Using several sizes of marble tile gives this floor a livelier look than one laid out on a strictly uniform grid. Light colors on the floor and in the cabinetry help the room feel spacious.

VINYL AND LAMINATE

Today's vinyl goes far beyond the wet and shiny look that once characterized this type of flooring. It's well suited for a bathroom—it's soft underfoot, isn't as cold to the touch as stone or tile, and is impervious to water. This makes it a particularly good choice for a child's bathroom, where you can bet that water from the tub or shower will make its way to the floor regularly. Vinyl can be installed over another layer of resilient flooring, as long as it's well bonded, or over an existing wood floor with the addition of a layer of plywood underlayment, making it a good choice for a partial remodel where the existing floor is not removed.

Laminate flooring, designed as a "floating" floor system, consists of a fiberboard core topped by a printed image (typically of wood grain) and protected by a clear layer of plastic resin called the wear layer. Although laminate flooring mimics the appearance of natural materials, it's thinner than conventional wood flooring and feels different underfoot. It also can't be refinished.

The biggest advantage to using laminate flooring in a bathroom remodel is that it can be installed over existing floors—vinyl, concrete, and hardwood, for example—as long as the manufacturer's directions are followed. But beware: If this type of flooring is used in a bathroom, edges around toilets, tubs, and sinks must be sealed carefully with silicone caulk to prevent damage. Shower curtains or doors should be used faithfully, and any pooled water should be mopped up promptly so that water doesn't seep through the flooring's snap-together seams and damage its fiberboard core.

above • With so many color choices in resilient flooring, it's easy to make any floor plan seem elegant and sophisticated.

facing page top • Vinyl tile is economical and easy to install. Up-to-date design options make this a stylish choice as well.

facing page bottom • Laminate flooring can be manufactured to look like many types of flooring, including ceramic tile.

left • With the look of ceramic tile, a vinyl floor is less expensive, more resilient, and impervious to water.

SOLID WOOD AND ENGINEERED WOOD

Wood flooring can be anything from traditional American hardwoods like cherry, maple, and oak to tropical species and even bamboo (actually a grass). Wood makes excellent flooring but it doesn't react well to water, so its use in the bathroom is risky. Wood flooring comes in two basic varieties: solid boards, which can be wide square-edged planks or tongue-and-groove strip flooring, and the more recent engineered varieties that are made by gluing thin layers of wood together to form plywood-like boards.

Solid and engineered wood flooring is available in many species and in a wide price range. Lower grades of solid wood flooring are less expensive than engineered wood flooring, but both can range up to $10 or so per square foot. Solid wood is a traditional flooring material so it shows up in plenty of bathrooms in older homes, but moisture will damage the finish and eventually degrade the wood itself to the point where it must be pulled up and replaced. Wood also expands as it absorbs water and contracts as moisture levels drop, meaning it's less dimensionally stable than engineered wood.

Despite its disadvantages around water and high humidity, wood flooring looks entirely appropriate in some bathrooms. An Adirondack-style cabin is right at home with fir-strip flooring in a warm amber color. Likewise, you'd expect to find wide-plank pine flooring in the bathroom of a New England farmhouse from the 18th century, even if the choice isn't the most practical one. Wood also can be a good choice for a refurbished powder room where water isn't as much of an issue as in a full bath.

Cork

Cork flooring comes from the bark of a tree that can be harvested once every 10 years without doing any damage to the tree. That makes it an appealingly green material. It's also very comfortable to walk on because each cubic inch of cork contains millions of tiny air bubbles. Among cork's other attributes are that it feels warm under bare feet, it's hypoallergenic, it deadens sound, and it acts as a thermal insulator.

But like other wood products, cork swells when it comes into contact with water, so using it in a bathroom carries the same risks as other water-sensitive materials. If you decide to use cork flooring in a bathroom, choose glue-down parquet tile rather than a tongue-and-groove floating floor system, because the parquet tiles are less susceptible to water damage. Regardless, all flooring made of cork should be sealed with an industrial-grade water-based polyurethane finish after installation to keep water out of the seams.

top • The blond wood flooring in this bathroom doesn't fight with the design of the vanity and tub surround and helps the space feel spacious and open.

above • Wood flooring looks exactly right in homes built before the introduction of ceramic tile, vinyl, and other more contemporary materials.

left • The area rug provides color and floor warmth in this traditional bathroom full of white fixtures and wainscot.

Walls and Ceilings

What makes the right wall covering or treatment in a bathroom is a combination of factors: how the room will be used, whether it's a full bath or a powder room, whether the bathroom was remodeled, including the removal of existing wall surfaces, and, of course, the look and feel you're trying to achieve. Materials that can be used here include gypsum drywall, plaster, tile, and wood. Costs vary considerably.

When renovating a newer house it makes sense to leave walls and ceilings undisturbed, provided they are in good condition to start with. But the added mess and expense of a tearout is a good idea when insulation is missing or inadequate, when there are signs of water damage, or when there's no other way to add an exhaust fan. The question gets more complicated in historically valuable houses where original plaster, molding, or other features are worth protecting. But two things are generally true in any remodeling project. First, it's easier in the long run to tear out the old if repairs are going to be extensive. Second, never cover up structural weakness or water-damaged materials with new work. It won't last.

top right • Vertical wood planks make a contemporary wainscoting in this bathroom. Naturally resilient to the touch, wood makes a durable wall covering in this application.

above • Wallpaper can be a dramatic design tool, filling this small bathroom with color and pattern.

right • Wood walls can feel warm, but here the effect is more rustic thanks to exposed wood timbers and a mirror detailed in birch bark.

Pale green mosaics with blue accents make for a more interesting wall than either color would by itself.

Covering Walls and Ceilings

A bathroom can be a tough environment for walls and ceilings as well as floors. High levels of humidity in bathrooms with showers but without exhaust fans and direct exposure to water will damage some materials more readily than others. In general, the most durable materials are also the most expensive to install.

GYPSUM DRYWALL
$

- When painted, it's a low-cost way of making a high-impact change in a bathroom that needs minor alterations rather than an extensive overhaul.
- Relatively inexpensive.
- Don't use in areas directly exposed to water, such as shower walls.
- More susceptible to nicks and dings than tile, wood, or stone.
- Water-resistant variety can be used on ceilings of showers.

TILE AND STONE
$$–$$$

- Extremely durable.
- Impervious to water. Can be used on shower walls and tub surrounds.
- Great variety of textures, colors, and sizes available for excellent design flexibility.
- A natural material with a lot of eye appeal.
- Expensive and difficult to change once installed, and more expensive than most other surfaces.

WOOD AND WOOD LOOK-ALIKES
$–$$

- A flexible material that can be applied in many ways and painted, stained, or protected by a clear-coat finish without changing its natural color.
- A variety of wood species and engineered wood products are available, including plastic look-alikes that resemble traditional wood beadboard.
- A naturally resilient material that's more durable than wallpaper and gypsum drywall but not as tough as tile or stone.
- Easy and inexpensive to repaint or recoat.
- Should be protected from direct contact with excessive amounts of water.

WOOD

TILE

DRYWALL

A log house provides its own finish walls inside.
The look is warm and rustic.

Those basics out of the way, a good first step in narrowing the choices for walls and ceilings is to consider who will be using the bathroom and how often it will be used. Attractive but delicate wallpaper might be appropriate in a powder room mainly used by guests, for example, but risky in a bathroom where small children regularly wash their hands. Choices also will be dictated by materials found elsewhere in the house or by its overall architectural style, such as Arts and Crafts, Colonial, or rustic. Finally, it makes sense to consider walls and ceilings together rather than as unrelated design elements. These two surfaces can complement each other, and in the hands of a skilled designer used in tandem to alter the perception of a room's size and ceiling height. (Finishes such as wallpaper and paint are covered in Finishing Touches, beginning on p. 194.)

above • Tile wainscoting is a durable easy-to-clean surface that has a more formal look than wood or drywall.

left • Wood bead board capped by a simple chair rail lends a casual feel to a room. When using wainscot, be sure it comes up high enough behind the sink to act as a backsplash and protect the other wall coverings.

TILE AND STONE

Ceramic tile and stone are as durable on walls as they are on floors. They are easy to keep clean, resist water damage, and offer a tremendous amount of design flexibility. Tile is especially versatile. Different shapes, patterns, and colors can be mixed to create striking field patterns, chair rails, and baseboards. Even with its natural veining, stone often presents a more subdued face than tile, but its natural textures and strong colors can be dramatic when used on a wall. Slate, limestone, and marble all are good choices, although their various textures and colors will produce different effects.

right • A slate vanity top with a matching floor is elegant as well as long-wearing and makes a dramatic contrast with light-colored wood.

below • The many faces of glass and ceramic tile make it easy to achieve a custom look.

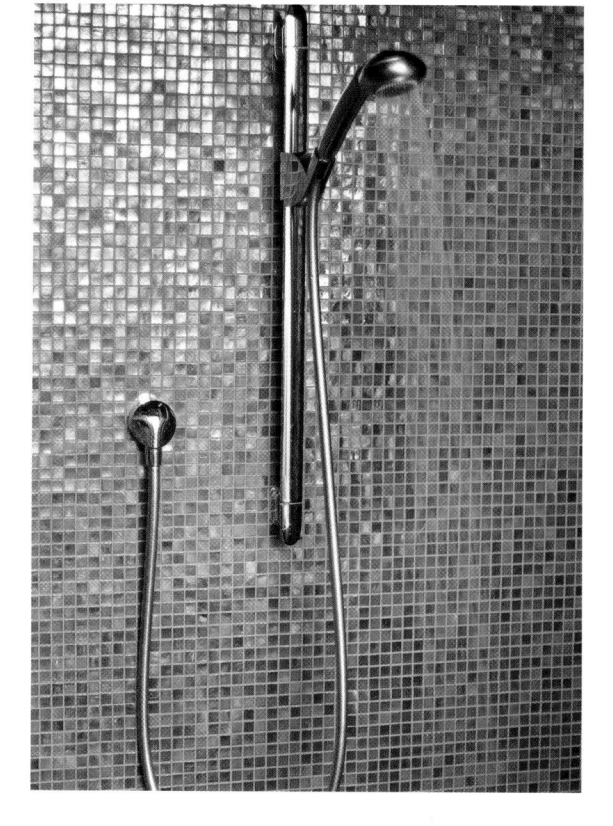

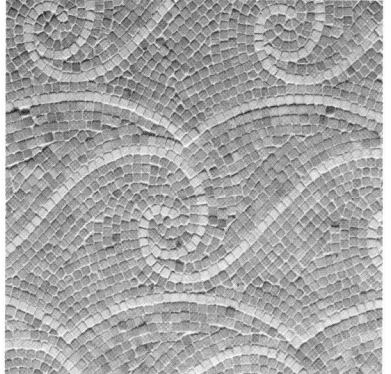

Trim and accent tiles make up a small percentage of the total used in this bathroom, but they make a big impact.

Tile or stone can be used to form the baseboard at the bottom of a wall or carried up the walls to form wainscoting. Because the choice of tile is virtually unlimited, so are the possibilities for tile wainscoting. Field tile can be capped with a variety of accent or border tiles to create bold chair rails, or it can be carried all the way to the ceiling. To unify the room visually, carry a band of accent tiles at chair-rail height around the perimeter of the bathroom, including the shower. You can keep the cost of tile down by using mostly economically priced tile on the walls and dressing it up occasionally with a more interesting and more expensive accent tile. Using narrow bands of glass tile, for example, or scattering handmade tiles throughout a field of plain white tiles can enliven otherwise ordinary walls.

Because it's not susceptible to moisture damage and it's easy to clean, tile wainscoting is especially good in bathrooms used by kids, particularly boys. On the downside, tile can look and feel cold and it reflects sound. Finally, tile, unlike paint, is very expensive to replace when you get tired of the color or pattern.

top right • Tile can be used on just about any surface. When the same colored tile is combined in different patterns and shapes it brings an unusual degree of continuity to a room.

facing page • A checkerboard border and accent tiles of the same color provide just enough contrast on a field of white tile.

Wainscoting with Flair

This bathroom is a good example of mixing materials but keeping colors in the same family to create a sense of visual continuity. Painted drywall with wainscoting made of tumbled marble fits the historic home's Spanish Colonial theme. The tile pattern, including its contrasting upper border, is carried right into the shower to unify the room visually. Wall colors are picked up in the glazed finish of the vanity and storage cabinets that flank the mirror above the countertop.

WOOD AND WOOD LOOK-ALIKES

Painted, stained, or left its natural color, wood can be a relatively inexpensive wall covering that offers a good number of design possibilities to suit a variety of tastes and architectural styles. It can run either horizontally or vertically, or be made into frame-and-panel wainscoting and capped with a chair rail.

If you prefer wood that's left its natural color, be prepared to spend a little more money to get it—the best grades are expensive, although the natural patina that wood develops over time can't be matched by any other material. Even the best grades of wood have a more casual feel than materials like stone or tile, whereas grades with more knots and surface defects can be appealing in rustic or period bathrooms.

One thing to keep in mind about wood is that it shrinks and expands in response to humidity, so it should be protected against direct exposure to water. Even when protected by top-quality clear finishes or paint, wood really isn't a good choice for wet areas like shower walls or tub surrounds.

If you're worried about moisture's long-term effect on wood or engineered wood products, consider a cellular PVC product, which is impervious to moisture and looks like traditional painted beadboard.

right • The exposed roof framing and sheathing painted a uniform white, along with an old-fashioned slipper tub, help to give this bathroom appealing cottagelike charm.

top right, facing page • Rich wood paneling in this tiny bathroom flows seamlessly from walls to vanity. Even the grain patterns seem to match.

top left, facing page • The designer of this renovated Vermont dairy barn used wood on the ceiling in keeping with an authentic period look.

bottom facing page • Wood wainscoting normally doesn't extend this far up the wall, but here it makes the room look larger. The band of deep red between wainscoting and ceiling is a dramatic accent.

Creating a Period Look in a New Bathroom

The challenge was to turn a small second-floor bedroom into a bathroom with a look that matched the Dutch Colonial architecture of the house. A first step was stripping the room in this Longmeadow, Mass., home to the framing and tapping into existing water-supply and drain lines that served the adjacent master bathroom. Then came fixtures and detailing to create a modern bath that didn't feel out of place.

Beadboard wainscoting was made from medium-density fiberboard (MDF), a manmade material that is stable and holds paint well. A custom-built cabinet reminiscent of a period built-in took the place of a small closet. It's built to follow the slope of the steeply pitched gambrel roof, with a pair of inset doors opening to shallow storage above and a bank of drawers taking advantage of deeper space below.

Although the owners had considered an electric radiant floor heating system, they opted to save a little money by repainting an existing radiator, another detail that helps retain the feel of an older house. The floor is made from small hexagonal tile, which is carried over into the three-sided shower. Finally, period-style sconces on either side of the medicine chest round out the room's new-old look.

top · A built-in cabinet takes advantage of a steeply pitched gambrel roof with deep drawers below and shelves above. The bin-pull drawer hardware has a period look in keeping with the Dutch Colonial style of the house.

right · Beadboard wainscoting, small hexagonal floor tile, and a painted radiator all contribute to the bathroom's period look.

facing page · A pedestal sink with a fluted base is an attractive alternative to a heavy vanity cabinet. The chair rail capping the wainscoting and the wall-mounted medicine cabinet are nicely balanced details in the room.

LIGHTING

Lighting provides color, evokes moods, and dramatizes

surfaces and textures. How and where it's used can make all the

difference between a bathroom that really works and one that doesn't.

Good lighting is created by a series of "layers" that provide different kinds of lights for different purposes. In addition to natural light provided by windows or skylights, there's light for tasks such as grooming or bathing, for finding your way around at night, for setting a mood, or maybe just to emphasize a special feature in the room.

Designers separate lighting into three categories:

- **Ambient lighting:** General lighting that's often provided by a single fixture in the ceiling or on the wall.

- **Task lighting:** Around the vanity and mirror or in the shower, this provides concentrated light for grooming and bathing.

- **Accent lighting:** Intended to highlight a feature of the room but not become a feature itself.

A bathroom can also feature decorative lighting, which provides some general light, though it's really intended to be a visual complement to the room, such as a decorative wall sconce. And who wouldn't want natural light in their bathroom? A window or skylight can make even the smallest bathroom feel a bit more spacious.

There are also special bathtubs with tiny light fixtures mounted right in the tub walls, an entirely different kind of bathroom lighting.

top • **A pair of lights mounted at about eye level will cast plenty of light without creating shadows on the face. Incandescent bulbs provide a warm, yellowish light.**

top right • **Lights mounted directly over the mirror are another option, although they can produce more shadows on the face.**

right • **Natural light makes pleasant ambient lighting in a bathroom. When turned on, the eyeball light above the tub will make it a focal point.**

facing page • **This shower has both a small window and an overhead lighting fixture for a nice mix of different kinds of light. Both are reflected by the glass walls.**

Although the fixture is typically what gets the most notice, the light bulb is what really makes the difference. A light bulb can be one of several types—fluorescent, incandescent, or halogen, low voltage or line voltage—all of which may cast different kinds of light. Bulbs also vary widely in cost, durability, and the amount of energy they consume.

Consider also a dimmer for your bath. You'll need to be sure a dimmer is compatible with the kind of light you're installing, but having one is a great way to change the mood of the room and extend bulb life.

left • The lighting scheme over the twin sinks here works well because the mirror is illuminated on both sides and each sink has a light focused directly on it.

facing page • Powerful recessed task lighting throws ample light in this oversize shower, a benefit in a bathroom where natural light is subdued by stained glass.

Light Bulbs

The light bulb, or "lamp" as it's called in the trade, has the biggest impact on the quality of light in the room. The most common types are conventional incandescents, halogens, and fluorescents, but there are a lot of variations on these basic themes. Variables include the cost of the bulbs, how long they last, and how much light the bulbs cast per unit of electricity they consume.

STANDARD INCANDESCENTS
$

- Inexpensive and available everywhere.
- Relatively short-lived, typically less than 1,000 hours.
- Very little of the electrical energy that incandescents consume is turned into light; most is thrown off as heat.

- Although inefficient, incandescents make good general lighting in a bathroom and are often recommended for vanity task lighting because the light is warm and complementary to skin tones.

HALOGENS
$$

- Similar to conventional incandescents, but burn hotter, last longer, and are more expensive.
- Generate considerable heat.
- Produce crisp, white light.
- Low-voltage fixtures are usually quite small and unobtrusive and are excellent for accent lighting.

FLUORESCENTS
$$

- Produce significantly more light per watt of energy than incandescents or halogens. A 32-watt fluorescent tube will produce nearly four times the amount of light as a 60-watt incandescent bulb.

- Last 20 times as long as conventional incandescent bulbs.
- Available as compact lights that fit in standard light sockets.
- Color rendering more accurate than in the past.
- Fixtures are more limited than those for incandescent bulbs and can be pricey.

LOW-VOLTAGE LIGHTS
$$$

- Most reduce 120-volt line current to 12 volts with a built-in or remote transformer.
- Fixtures cost roughly two to four times as much as conventional ones but are less expensive to operate.
- Bulbs last longer than standard incandescents.

Ambient Lighting

As its name suggests, ambient (or general) lighting is background lighting designed to get you around the room. Natural light, one type of general lighting, can be provided by a window, skylight, or solar tube, a variation on a conventional skylight that pipes sunlight down a reflective tube and broadcasts it from a ceiling-mounted dome. Although very large bathrooms may need multiple fixtures, ambient lighting is usually provided by a single dominant fixture that's either mounted on the wall or suspended from the ceiling. This fixture can be thought of as the "eye candy" of the room, setting the tone for lighting fixtures elsewhere in the space.

Incandescent bulbs with their characteristically warm yellowish light are the best and most common choice for ambient lighting. Halogen bulbs cast a brighter and whiter light. Although fluorescent lights have a bad reputation for casting cold or unpleasant light, the latest types now can mimic natural light, plus they are highly energy efficient, producing more light for the same amount of electricity as incandescents.

Just how much ambient lighting you need depends on the size of your room. An industry formula suggests 1 watt of incandescent light per square foot of floor area, with twice that much for halogen fixtures and one-third to one-half that amount for fluorescents. But factors such as wall color, ceiling height, and the amount of natural light streaming into the space can change those numbers.

right • No one said bathroom lights have to be staid and boring. In a large room with high ceilings, a chandelier casts good general lighting; this one also adds flair to the room.

facing page • Track lighting is a good option because light heads are easily moved or added based on the design of the room. It works well in this bathroom because it allows one style of lighting to be used for multiple tasks.

Light by Numbers

Thanks to the work of 19th-century Scottish physicist and engineer William Thomson (better known as Lord Kelvin), light from an incandescent bulb is now measured in kelvins, a scale that determines whether colors look "warm" or "cool." Lower color temperatures correspond with warmer yellows and reds and complement skin tones, whereas higher color temperatures correspond to cooler light with more bluish hues.

Another set of numbers is called the Color Rendering Index, which measures the ability of light to render colors accurately. The scale runs from 1 to 100; the higher the number, the better the color accuracy of the light source.

Task Lighting

Lighting around the vanity and mirror is probably the most critical in the room. After all, it's here where we groom ourselves for the day, brushing our hair and teeth, applying makeup, or shaving.

A pair of lights, one on either side of the mirror, is what works best. When positioned about 30 in. apart and at eye level, the light projects outward, lighting the face evenly. In larger bathrooms with a double-sink vanity, two pairs of fixtures, one for each mirror, or a third fixture set midway between the two mirrors may be necessary.

Because incandescent bulbs cast a warm, flattering light, they are a good choice for fixtures located on either side of a vanity mirror. Ideally, bulbs should be anywhere from 60 to 100 watts, though putting fixtures on dimmer switches and using higher-wattage bulbs provides a wider range of lighting levels.

Fluorescent bulbs provide more diffuse light than standard incandescents or halogens. Because the entire tube lights up, they cast fewer shadows.

right • Fitting the contemporary styling of this bathroom, these swooping low-voltage fixtures are adjustable as well as fun to look at. Lighting heads closer to the ceiling provide general room lighting.

Natural Light from Above

This bathroom demonstrates how effective a skylight can be in augmenting conventional lighting fixtures. On a bright day no other lighting would be needed. Yet around the sink task lighting is essential for applying makeup or shaving. Mixing different types of light for different purposes is the hallmark of a good lighting plan.

bottom left • These shaded wall sconces fit the décor of this bathroom nicely while still providing effective task lighting at the mirror.

bottom right • This bathroom effectively uses a mix of lighting—natural light from a row of transom windows that preserve privacy and a pair of fixtures that provide effective task lighting at the mirror. Light is thrown from both the top and bottom of the fixtures.

PUTTING IT ALL TOGETHER

Adding Light with Privacy in Mind

Opaque glass block set vertically in an interior bathroom wall brings an unusual source of light into the shower while protecting privacy at the same time. The glass door of the wall cabinet has the same effect. On the outside of the bathroom the glass block becomes an interesting design element.

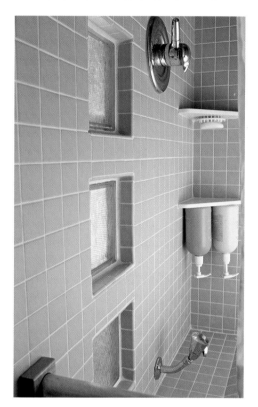

above • **Opaque glass block climbs up the wall of this shower enclosure, bringing light in without sacrificing privacy.**

right • **From the outside of the bathroom the block has a decorative effect.**

A fixture mounted directly over the mirror and projecting light outward rather than down is another choice to consider around the vanity, and it may be a more practical one for bathroom remodels of limited scope. Suppose, for example, that the wall over the sink is filled entirely with a mirror. Although it's possible to mount a pair of fixtures on the glass, it's expensive, so a hanging fixture can prove to be an attractive, more affordable option.

In the shower, a vapor-proof recessed or surface fixture makes it a lot easier to see what you're doing. Fixtures for low-voltage halogens can be relatively small and unobtrusive, and the bright white light they produce makes for excellent visibility. Shower fixtures must be approved for wet locations, and exposed bulbs are not permitted by code.

above • Undercabinet light fixtures throw a soft glow and produce effective accent lighting. The ceiling fixtures offer more general lighting of the space.

left • Two kinds of task lighting, adjustable track lights over the sink and a dedicated shower fixture, keep things clear in this bathroom.

Accent Lighting

If ambient and task lighting do most of the heavy work in a bathroom lighting plan, accent lighting can put architectural features or artwork on display. Sometimes referred to as the "third zone," accent lighting calls attention to a particular feature in a room.

Accent lights used in other rooms in the house don't function well in the bathroom because they're too big for the bathroom's smaller size. Small recessed fixtures, less than 6 in. in diameter, will do well in the bathroom because they focus low-voltage halogen light on features you want to emphasize without drawing as much attention to the fixture itself. One type of low-voltage halogen fixture, called a "pinhole" or "slot," focuses light very precisely. To keep accent lights from becoming the star players in a lighting plan, you can paint recessed fixtures so they blend in with the ceiling.

top left • Double hanging lights offer task lighting in an unusual though effective way. Because the light fixtures are open on the bottom, light is cast on either side of the mirror, just where you want it when grooming.

top right • A vapor-proof fixture in the shower is effective task lighting, especially when part of the stall is tucked into a corner and would otherwise be dark.

Hiring a Lighting Designer

There may be some valuable advice on lighting available locally and for free. Check with the American Lighting Association (www.american lightingassoc.com) to get the names of member showrooms and consultants. House of Lights, a showroom I visited in Scarborough, Maine, was offering free hour-long consultations in the showroom. An on-site visit where a lighting designer visits the house and devises a customized lighting plan cost $150, but the fee is credited back to buyers who spend more than $1,000 in fixtures.

The wall-mounted lighting fixture here offers true accent light. With ample natural light flooding into this bathroom, more minimal artificial light is successful.

This large expanse of countertop is bathed in light thanks to triple light fixtures over each sink. The large overhead fixture provides good general lighting, whereas the recessed fixture over the tub provides task lighting in that area.

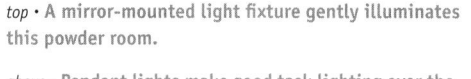

top • A mirror-mounted light fixture gently illuminates this powder room.

above • Pendant lights make good task lighting over the vanity but when used alone can cast shadows on the face.

left • Accent lighting, like that hidden above crown molding here, can do double duty as a night light.

Accent lighting also can come from rope lights, fluorescents, or low-voltage halogens concealed in a trough. Depending on where they're placed, upward-facing fixtures will wash a spot on the wall or the ceiling with light and cast enough reflected light into the room to create a pleasant glow and help to set a mood. When used underneath a cabinet that is suspended from the wall, accent light will add drama to the space.

Light in the Tub

If a tub full of hot water isn't enough, you may want to look into a tub that combines air or water jets with light-emitting diodes (LEDs) that turn bathwater different colors. Manufacturers call the combination of water and color by different tradenames, but most claim that different color lights can evoke different moods in the bather. White, for example, is said to be pure and clarifying, violet is inspiring and creative, yellow is hopeful and illuminating, and red is courageous and energizing.

left • Lighting fixtures can have a character all their own. Look for ones that reinforce a theme.

HEATING

Mechanical systems that control temperature and humidity in the bathroom should stay mostly out of sight and out of mind, but you'll notice instantly when they're not working.

AND

Choosing the right equipment keeps you comfortable no matter what the climate and ensures your house will stay healthy.

COOLING

Although equipment for heating, cooling, and controlling humidity isn't beautiful, it is a necessity. If you don't take the necessary steps to control the environment, moisture can cause long-term damage to your house. There are a range of options available, though it's best to consult a builder or heating and air-conditioning contractor to know exactly which mechanical devices are right for your house and your particular climate.

It's obvious when a room is either too hot or too cold, but moisture is a more insidious problem. Water that drips from a sweating toilet tank in steamy summer weather or leaks through improperly sealed tile grout is one kind of problem moisture. Another is airborne water vapor that begins in the bathtub, shower, or sink and infiltrates the ceiling and walls. Good building practices and the selection of quality building materials will help forestall both problems.

top right • Heat can come in many forms, not only conventional baseboard radiators, but also heating mats placed under flooring or even heating lamps mounted in the ceiling.

above • Due to the built-in cabinets there isn't a lot of room for heating and ventilation in the main section of this bathroom. The small window in the shower alcove helps dissipate moist air and offers air flow to the rest of the space.

right • A ceiling fan can be ordered as a fan only, as a light and fan combination, or with integral heating elements. Newer models are very quiet.

A fan placed close to a tub or shower will be more effective in removing moisture than one at the far end of a room.

Moisture wasn't much of an issue when houses were drafty and underinsulated, but it can be an issue today because of more stringent building codes, better materials, and a wider acceptance of energy-saving building techniques, all of which have resulted in houses that can easily trap moisture and humidity.

Regardless of what part of the country you live in, the idea is to prevent warm, moisture-laden air from coming into contact with a cool surface inside a wall cavity and to give walls and ceilings that do get damp a means of drying out. A combination of a vapor barrier on the walls and ventilating fans will keep moisture from being plugged up in the bathroom, and will help prevent mold and rot.

Containing water where it's supposed to be is another good way to ensure your bathroom remains sound. Caulking around tub and sink perimeters helps, but it's most important to make sure you install the bathroom fixtures that best fit your circumstances. A one-piece tub/shower is probably a smart choice in a child's bath, for instance, whereas a large soaking tub with little or no surround is better suited to an adult who won't be splashing around a lot.

Keeping Water in Its Place

Controlling water is the key to protecting walls, floors, and ceilings from long-term damage, but in a well-designed bathroom those measures blend into the background. Shower enclosures with high walls, snugly fitting doors, and an adequate curb will keep most of the water off the floor. Backsplashes around sinks will prevent water from running down the walls or getting trapped behind the sink or vanity. Tight grout or caulked joints keep water from going where it doesn't belong, and correctly sized ventilation fans remove water vapor before it can do any real harm.

Heat is another important factor for comfort. It can be provided by a half-dozen different systems, including toe-kick heaters installed beneath a vanity that stay out of sight.

above • A generous backsplash around the sink is another way of effectively controlling spills.

above • Old-fashioned radiators still throw plenty of heat and they look right at home in older homes. A radiator cover also offers added storage.

above • A pair of glass doors and a high curb will help keep water contained in the shower in this kid's bathroom, lessening the chance of water damage.

left • A heater installed beneath a cabinet can take the place of a conventional radiator while using less floor space. It blows warm air into the room through a vent in the cabinet's toekick.

Don't Skip the Fan

Once the walls are properly insulated and sealed, the most important step toward maintaining a healthy bathroom environment is to install a fan. Opening the window when you're showering or lounging in a tub is a help, but it isn't enough.

There are two basic types of bathroom fans: the familiar ceiling-mounted unit that may include a light or infrared bulb for supplemental heat, and inline fans that are installed some distance away, even on the roof.

No matter which kind of fan you settle on, two key considerations are how much noise it makes and how much air it's capable of moving. Inexpensive fans tend to rattle incessantly or hum loudly. Remote inline fans are typically a little louder than the best ceiling-mounted designs, although there are a variety of ways of muffling the noise.

The most effective place for a fan is in the ceiling, right over the area where damp air is generated. If you don't like the look of conventional grilles, vents can be hidden inside light fixtures. A fan can be installed in an exterior wall, but that's not as effective as having a fan with ceiling collectors, and it will probably make more noise; it's also likely that it will be more obvious.

Sizing a Bathroom Fan

Fan capacity is measured in cubic feet per minute (cfm) of air. For bathrooms up to 100 sq. ft., the industry rule of thumb is to allow 1 cfm for every square foot of floor area. When bathrooms are larger than that, other factors come into play. Enclosed water closets, bathtubs, and showers each need 50 cfm of fan capacity, whereas a whirlpool tub should have 100 cfm. Matching fan capacity to the design needs of the room should be easy, but remember that manufacturers arrive at the advertised specifications for their fans in near perfect laboratory conditions. Long runs of duct, using flexible duct, and including lots of bends and angles in the exhaust run all lower fan performance.

These shower walls extend all the way to the ceiling, keeping excess moisture out of the rest of the bathroom. A light/fan combination in the shower vents the area.

Bathroom Fans

STANDARD CEILING-MOUNTED FAN
$

- Most are installed so grille is exposed and nearly flush with the ceiling, although some are disguised as recessed lights with no visible grille.
- Picks up air from a single point.
- Discharges air through roof or an outside wall.
- Models available with built-in lights and heaters.
- Capable of extremely quiet operation.
- In large bathrooms with a whirlpool or separate toilet enclosure, more than one unit may be required.

INLINE REMOTE FAN
$$

- More expensive than most ceiling-mounted units, but able to move larger volume of air.
- Located away from the bathroom; can be mounted on the roof or an outside wall.
- Single fan can accommodate a number of pickup points in a single bathroom or provide ventilation for more than one bathroom.
- Makes more noise than the quietest ceiling-mounted model, but careful installation will minimize sound.
- Vents with built-in lights are available.

above • These ceiling-mounted fans look like recessed lights. The fan grate is completely concealed.

Timers and Sensors

Like any other feature in the bathroom, fan switches and controls can be selected to fit the way you live. For someone who runs out the door to work shortly after a morning shower and doesn't have time to wait while the fan does its job (count on at least 20 minutes), a timer is a good idea. More sophisticated switches can be programmed to cycle on and off throughout the day, and some are even designed to work as stand-in whole-house ventilators. Other types of switches sense humidity in the air and turn on the fan when it reaches a predetermined level. If you have absolutely no faith in your ability to remember to use the fan, there are motion-sensing versions available that will get the fan going as soon as you walk into the bathroom.

right • Sliding glass doors won't trap moisture as effectively as a full-height shower enclosure, but the location of a fan nearby will pick up steam and vapor.

Timers and Switches

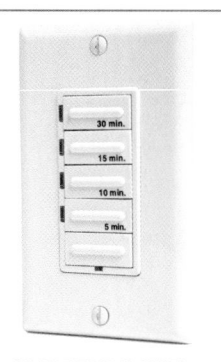

SIMPLE TIMING SWITCH

PROGRAMMABLE SWITCH

HUMIDITY-SENSING SWITCH

SIMPLE TIMING SWITCH
$

- Operates fan for specified length of time, then shuts off.
- May have separate buttons for different run times or time-delay switch that keeps fan running after it's been turned off.

PROGRAMMABLE SWITCH
$$

- Switch can be set to run automatically at different times of the day.
- Useful for controlling large remote fans used for whole-house ventilation.
- Some have adjustable air-flow rates, with a boost feature for full power during a shower.

HUMIDITY-SENSING SWITCH
$$$

- Can be set to turn fan on at a predetermined humidity level.
- Override feature allows fan to be turned on when showering regardless of humidity level.
- Automatic extraction of damp air, even when you forget to turn on the switch or turn the fan off too soon.

An unusual pivoting transom in this glass shower enclosure helps control the flow of air and moisture. A timer on the wall keeps a heat lamp in the shower warm.

Heat Sources

Unless your bathroom has an electrical heater with its own thermostat, chances are it's part of a heating zone that includes several other rooms, often some downstairs and some upstairs.

There are several options for improving an existing heating system. Adding a strip of electric baseboard heat or a heat-lamp fixture in the ceiling are relatively inexpensive ways of getting more heat in the bathroom without making any changes to the system that serves the rest of the house.

Installing an electric heating mat over an existing floor and capping that with tile is more labor intensive, but it does not require the removal of the floor you already have. Heating mats are very thin, so they don't affect the level of the floor very much, and are controlled by their own thermostats. Mats can be installed only under parts of the floor that you want to be warm underfoot—they're not intended as the sole source of heat.

above • A wall-mounted warmer keeps towels toasty and can provide some supplemental heat in the room.

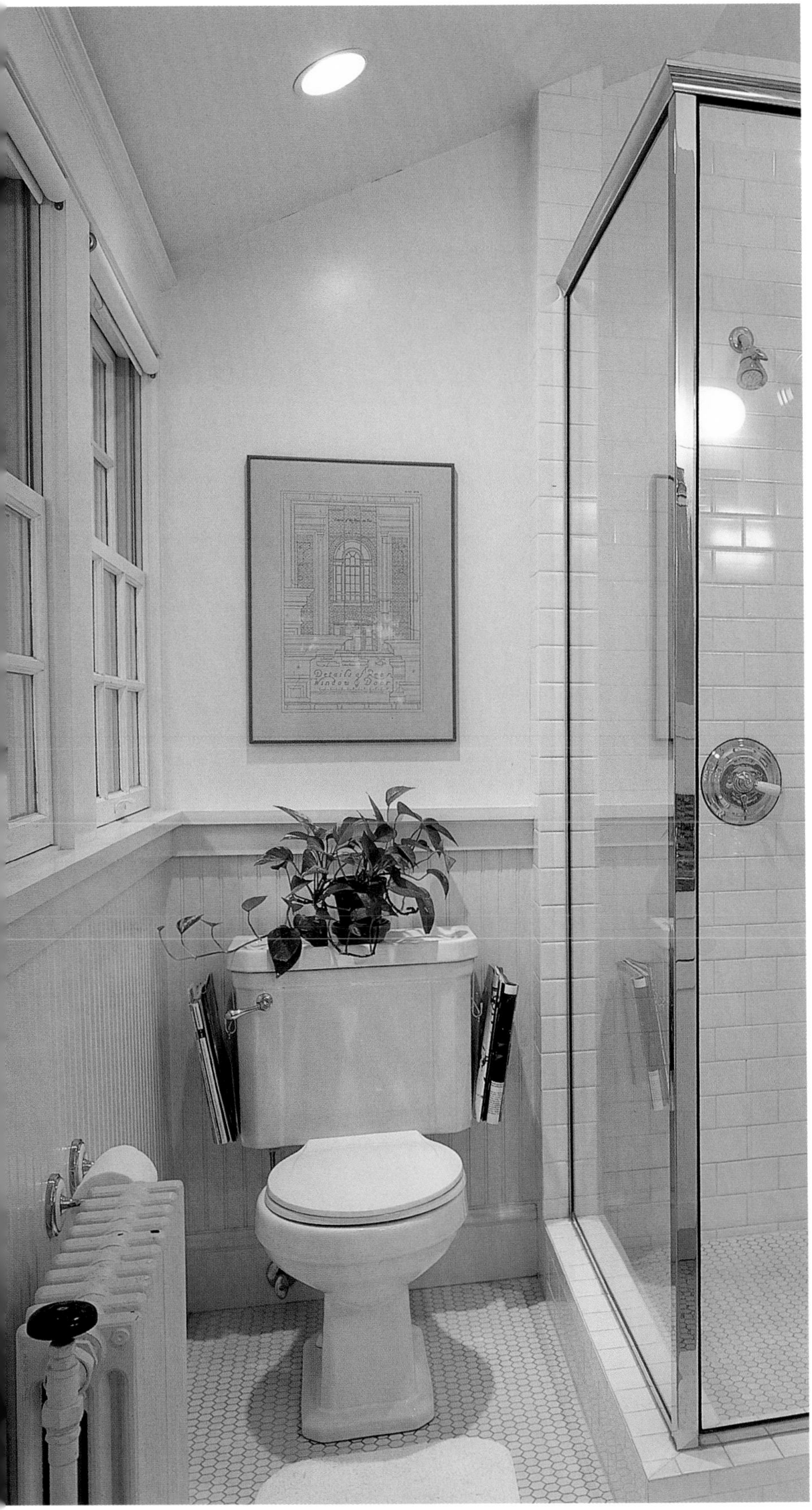

What's Loud?

In the world of appliances, sound is measured in something called a "sone" instead of the more familiar decibel. One sone is described as the amount of noise a quiet refrigerator makes in a quiet room. That is, not very much.

Unlike the more complex decibel system, sones are a linear scale—meaning, for example, that 4 sones is twice as much noise as 2 sones—and that makes it very easy for nonscientists to compare how much noise competing products make. Noise ratings are usually printed right on the box the fan comes in or should be readily available from the manufacturer.

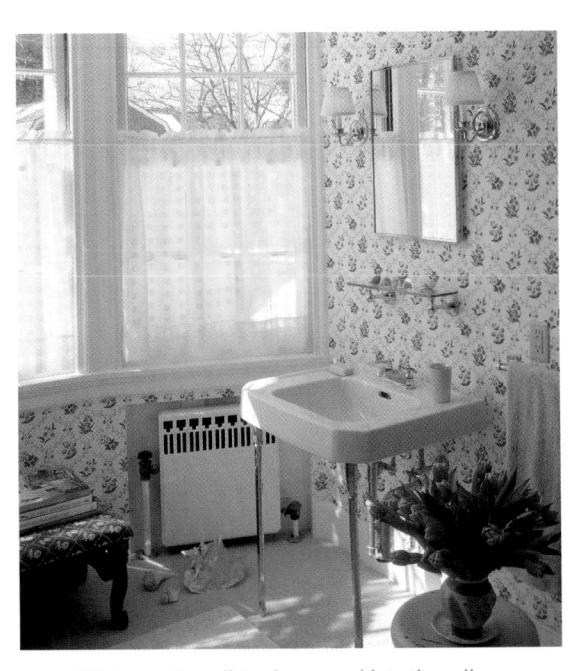

above • This hot-water radiator is recessed into the wall cavity, saving a bit of floor space but also making the wall more difficult to insulate.

left • Once the norm, cast iron radiators like this one have largely been replaced, but they'll still heat a room nicely.

facing page • The fan in this shower is unobtrusive and effective for both the shower and bathing area thanks to only a small glass-wall partition separating the shower from the vanity.

More elaborate modifications can include decorative wall radiator panels or even a hot-water radiant floor system on its own zone. Major alterations to an existing heating system—adding a dedicated hot-water zone in the bathroom for radiant floor heat, for example—make the most sense when floors and walls are opened up or during a whole-house renovation.

If you've got those old-fashioned cast iron radiators in the bathroom, they can become part of a period look or camouflaged with a manufactured or custom radiator cover. Radiator covers don't prevent the circulation of warm air in the room, and they also provide a convenient storage shelf. Because a radiator is often located right under a window, a cover becomes a good spot for a potted plant or the snoozing family cat.

right · Hot-water baseboard radiators are relatively inexpensive and don't take up much room. But they can rust, making them risky for use around a toilet.

Heaters

CEILING-MOUNTED HEAT LAMP
$

- One- and two-bulb models are available.
- Can be combined with a ventilation fan.
- Warmth comes from above, but floors can still be cold.
- Should be matched with a timer switch.

TOE-KICK SPACE HEATER
$–$$

- Fits in toekick beneath conventional cabinets, so it takes up no floor space.
- Electric and hydronic models available. Hydronic models work with hot-water heating systems and are harder to install during a remodel than electric units.
- Integral fans help boost heat output.
- Warms air but leaves floors cold.

WALL AND CEILING HEATER
$

- Doesn't intrude on floor space.
- A variety of heat outputs are available, drawing 120 or 240 volts.
- Integral fan circulates warm air.
- Relatively inexpensive, but limited color and material selection.

ELECTRIC RADIANT FLOOR MAT
$–$$

- Can be installed over existing floors, including sheet vinyl, and covered with new layer of flooring, usually tile.
- Thin profile makes minimal impact on floor thickness.
- Many standard sizes, but also can be made to custom shapes.
- Warms floor only in designated areas.

DECORATOR RADIATOR
$$$

- Sleeker, more attractive designs than conventional fin-tube baseboard heat.

- Available as wall panel, baseboard, and bench design.
- Can replace existing hydronic radiators without extensive plumbing changes.

RADIANT FLOOR HEAT
$$$

- Flooring must be removed for installation.
- Not an add-on to hot-air heating system; requires a hot-water boiler.
- No visible radiators.
- Floors stay warm.
- Provides stable, even heat.

TOWEL WARMER
$$

- Supplemental, not primary, heat in cold climates, but could be used to heat bathroom in milder climates.
- Keeps towels warm and dry and helps prevent mildew.
- Electric and hydronic versions available.

Radiators can be hidden with a simple cover that keeps all that cast iron out of sight but still allows warm air to circulate freely.

STORAGE

Few rooms in the house rival the bath as a place where we stock so

many necessities. Look beyond the standard medicine cabinet

and vanity to find creative storage solutions.

Whether a small powder room, large master bath, or midsize full bath shared by a family of five, every bathroom accumulates clutter. Somehow a place must be found to keep all the things you need at the moment, like tissues, soap, and towels, plus those that you pull out every so often.

Today's bathroom features updated versions of standard storage options—medicine chest, vanity, and shelf over the toilet—as well as freestanding furniture, open shelving, and hooks and holders. Used alone or in combination, any of these storage elements provides practicality as well as design opportunities, regardless of the size of the bathroom.

Bathroom cabinetry is more diverse and innovative than ever before. Some companies produce cabinets in sculptural shapes, and furniture-like vanities are now available from a number of manufacturers. A wide selection of shelf and drawer hardware makes it easy to customize cabinet interiors and make the most of storage space.

top right · Bathroom cabinetry that looks like furniture is gaining favor. Although it's always possible to convert small tables and bureaus into bathroom vanities, you can also choose among a growing number of factory-made pieces.

above · Twin medicine cabinets make personalized storage of toiletries easy. These cabinets combine open shelving with a conventional enclosure.

DETAILS THAT WORK

Built-In Bathroom Library

Well-planned bathroom storage meets the needs of its users—and that may mean finding a spot for reading material as well as towels and toiletries. This shallow wall niche next to the toilet is just big enough to hold several magazines. It's carefully detailed with marble, tile, and a brushed metal bar.

Bathroom cabinets can be sculptural as well as boxy, like this conical pedestal cabinet. The maple cabinet has a melamine interior.

What would have been unused space inside this wall cavity was turned into a recessed shelving unit. The location provides easy access to both the vanity and tub areas.

left · Narrow box-beam shelves on the wall of this tub area are a handy place for dry towels as well as toiletries. Using the same material for the shelves as for the wall creates a unified look.

far left · This occasional table fits snugly in a corner and the open frame makes useful towel storage.

Cabinets That Unify a Room

These shallow cabinets unify this bathroom while providing a lot of useful storage. Measuring only about 11 in. deep, the cabinets don't take up much floor space. The top of the cabinet blends seamlessly into trim that becomes window sill, chair rail, and backsplash at different points around the room.

The wraparound design encloses the tub and offers a sense of protection and privacy. Yet because the cabinets are painted white, they don't make the room feel closed in.

Open shelving beneath the sink countertop helps this narrow bathroom feel more spacious than would a solid cabinet front. Another open area lies behind the tub at the far end of the room, providing enough room to work tab valves comfortably as well as making room for a hanging towel.

Cabinets lining the wall of this renovated 1840s bathroom don't take up much room but offer about the same amount of storage as an average kitchen upper cabinet.

Cabinetry

Built-in bathroom cabinets are as varied as anything that's available for the kitchen, ranging from inexpensive, mass-produced boxes to showy and elaborately designed pieces of furniture. Cabinets also are built in a variety of styles, from French provincial to Arts and Crafts. Factory cabinets have traditionally fallen into one of three categories: stock, semi-custom, and custom.

STOCK

Stock cabinets are at the economy end of the scale. They are mass produced and available to take home the day you purchase them. With stock, what you see is what you get in terms of size and quality. Although colors, styles, wood types, and hardware are all limited, stock cabinets offer the opportunity to make an instant transformation without spending a lot of money.

SEMI-CUSTOM

Semi-custom cabinets represent a step up from stock, in terms of both quality and variety. As the name suggests, semi-custom cabinets offer more opportunities to customize the cabinets with accessories like corbels and crown molding, more complex glazed finishes, and a wider selection of doors and hardware. Both stock and semi-custom cabinets are built in 3-in. increments.

top • A drawer running the width of the cabinet beneath the doors increases storage options. The cabinet feet make this piece feel more like a piece of furniture than a standard vanity cabinet.

right • A custom piece like this beautifully detailed corner cabinet can become the elegant focal point in a bathroom, offering some storage but also unifying the room's design.

facing page • Zebra wood gives this bathroom vanity an unusually dramatic flair. The cabinet combines drawers with open shelving.

CUSTOM

Custom cabinets are made to order, which means you can get them built to any size and shape. Finish, trim, interior detailing, and materials all can be specified. Local cabinet shops are often the source for custom cabinets, although some larger manufacturers specialize in built-to-order cabinetry. While you'll get exactly the cabinets you want, be prepared to spend more money and wait longer to get them.

Another key difference is cabinet type. Like kitchen cabinets, bathroom cabinetry has until now been of two types: frameless, a carryover from European design, or traditional face frame. Although those boxy styles are still dominant, there are many more choices in manufactured lines, ranging from more sculpturally shaped pedestals and base cabinets to vanities that on first glance look like a bombé chest or a Sheraton table.

top right • These mirror-image cabinets are ideal for a shared master bath. Elevating them off the floor makes them seem less bulky.

above • This long cabinet installation packs a lot of punch, offering three banks of drawers separated by two other compartments with doors.

right • When base cabinets are held off the floor by more than the amount of a standard toe kick they don't look boxy or imposing. Accent lighting installed beneath the cabinet makes the effect even more dramatic.

The rich color of the wood used in these cabinets becomes a dominant design element of the room. The simple yet bold hardware enhances the cabinetry.

Although this sink is of a normal depth, the cabinet in which it's installed is narrower than usual, reducing its bulk and allowing the bathroom to feel more spacious.

Cabinet Types

Manufactured cabinets come in a variety of styles, price ranges, and materials. They have historically been divided into three broad categories—stock, semi-custom, and custom—to help distinguish their features, finishes, and options.

STOCK
$

- Built in increments of 3 in.
- Stocked by home centers and bath and kitchen showrooms and ready to sell, so they can be picked up and installed the same day you buy them.
- Limited selection of styles, finishes, and wood types.
- Fewer options on hardware than semi-custom or custom lines.
- Building materials tend to be less durable than those used in more expensive lines—vinyl-covered particleboard instead of solid lumber or plywood, for example.

SEMI-CUSTOM
$$

- Also built in increments of 3 in.
- Ordered through home centers or showrooms. Delivery may take some weeks.
- More options available for finishes, trim, wood types, and hardware.
- Building materials and techniques tend to be of higher quality: dovetailed drawers instead of doweled or stapled joints, for example, and more plywood rather than particleboard.
- Better selection of cabinet pulls and hardware.

CUSTOM
$$$

- Built completely to order, so cabinets can be made to fill any space exactly without the use of filler strips.
- Can be ordered from specialized manufacturers or through local cabinet and millwork shops.
- Extended lead times typical from small shops, so cabinets must be ordered well in advance.
- Finish can be matched to any desired color or texture.
- Should expect the best materials and building techniques to be used.
- Virtually any wood species or hardware may be ordered.

top • These custom wall cabinets were designed for a homeowner who liked rectangular shapes. The solid wood and plywood boxes are 10 in. deep and use spring latches and concealed hinges.

above • With a desklike knee space, this bathroom vanity doubles as a dressing table.

Traditionally built cabinets sit on a base about 4 in. high that forms a toe kick. This prevents an awkward back strain when you get right next to the cabinet to use the counter. But cabinets also can be mounted directly to the wall, leaving the space beneath them wide open. The cabinets still provide substantial storage, but they don't look as if they're hogging as much space as ones that go all the way to the floor. The illusion of more space can be enhanced by adding accent lighting beneath the cabinet.

Another way of getting something a little different is by mixing and matching cabinet components or working with a custom shop to assemble a wall or even a roomful of cabinets. Obviously, how many and what size cabinets will vary based on the size of your bathroom, but don't discount this approach, even if your bathroom seems small.

top right • In a unique curved configuration, this run of cabinetry is further enhanced by a bold stroke of color in the drawers, a simple but effective decorative technique.

above • This bathroom gets ample above-counter storage with these two glass-fronted cabinets, a smart detail in a shared bathroom.

right • Breaking a few rules can produce cabinetry that catches the eye. The interesting angular shape means the vanity is less bulky than a conventional cabinet would be.

Even though this cabinet is raised off the floor, it doesn't lose any storage thanks to the ample drawers and shelves behind the door.

Bathroom Cabinets

Whether you opt for custom or off-the-shelf cabinetry, there's plenty to choose from. Cabinets can be designed to complement a room of virtually any size, shape, or architectural style, adding visual appeal as well as providing needed storage. By choosing cabinet colors and materials carefully, you'll add your personality to the room. If you're tall, consider cabinets 36 in. high, the same as standard kitchen cabinets, to reduce back strain.

1. When space allows, adding a dressing table provides practicality as well as opportunity for storage, as witnessed by this floor-to-ceiling frameless cabinet. **2.** Sleek and contemporary, this built-in provides a generous amount of storage. Its slender door pulls are a good match with the lighting, wall-mounted faucets, and mirrored walls. **3.** A frameless cabinet design shows only drawer fronts and doors on the face, a more contemporary look than conventional face-frame cabinets.

4. Face-frame cabinets look more like traditional furniture than frameless designs. These cabinets are enlivened with a textural door front, enhancing the earthy tone of this bathroom. 5. Drawer fronts can be solid pieces of wood or frame-and-panel pieces, as shown here. Frame and panel is a more traditional look than a solid front. 6. A large sink tops this cherry and mahogany base cabinet, giving the vanity a much more contemporary look than traditional bathroom built-ins.

Rejuvenated Bath

The new owners of a 1920s cottage-style house on Bainbridge Island, Wash., decided to stick with the same footprint when they overhauled this second-floor bathroom. That decision helped to keep costs under control but created a challenge for the project's architect.

With the help of two strategically located pocket doors, the rejuvenated bath can be used simultaneously as a powder room and a bathing area and is accessible from the adjacent master bedroom or the hallway. The arrangement provides two separate vanities for storage, one in the bathing area next to the new shower and a second one in the half-bath area near the hall.

The design called for the replacement of a large jetted tub with a walk-in shower, illuminated by a skylight that brings a generous amount of natural light into the room. A glass shower enclosure prevents the small room from feeling cramped.

The end result is a bathroom that's more efficient, brighter, and more comfortable. Careful selection of materials helps.

BEFORE

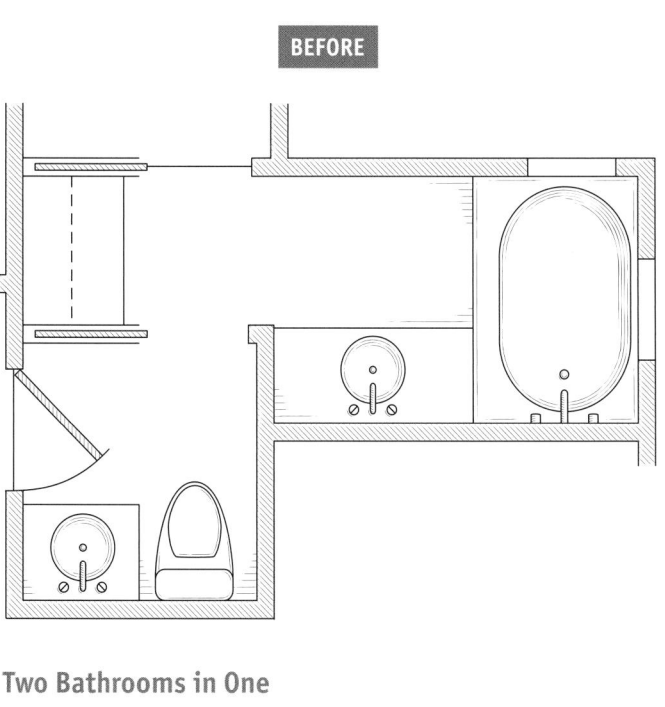

Two Bathrooms in One

Using the same footprint saved money, but adding light and new finishes revived the bathroom. One major change in this dual-purpose bathroom was swapping a walk-in shower for an outdated jetted tub.

AFTER

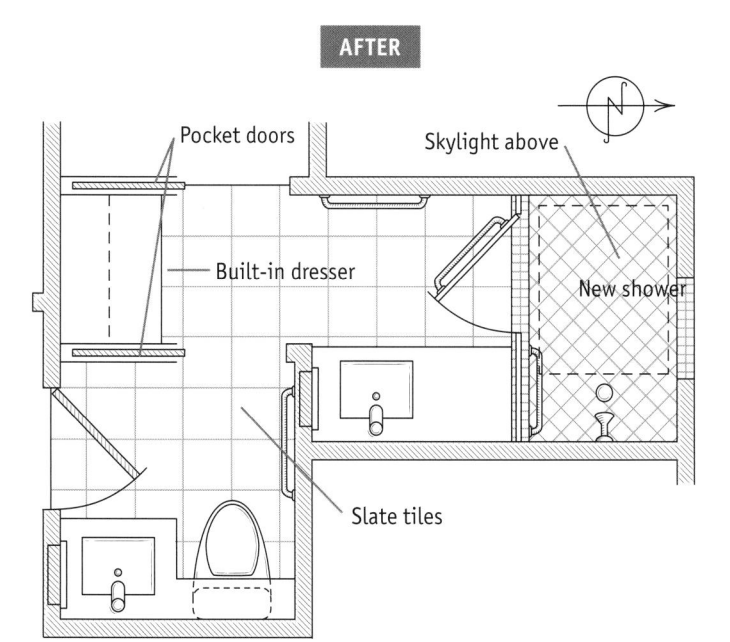

Pocket doors

Skylight above

Built-in dresser

New shower

Slate tiles

top · A large mirror helps this small space seem larger. This half-bath is accessible from an adjacent hall even as the shower side is being used by someone else.

left · A new skylight in this remodeled bath brightens up the walk-in shower lined with sparkling glass tiles.

MEDICINE CABINETS

Medicine cabinets are especially useful in bathrooms with pedestal sinks, because storage is often limited. If you've grown used to doing battle with an old medicine chest recessed into the wall (you know, the one with the sliding doors that jump their tracks and a built-in fluorescent fixture behind a piece of yellowing plastic), you might be surprised to see the new generation of wall cabinets now on the market, with features that enliven this standard bathroom cabinet: doors with ribbed glass or no-fog mirrors, built in electrical outlets, and pull-out makeup mirrors.

Medicine cabinets are either surface mounted or recessed into the wall. A recessed cabinet intrudes less into the room while still providing ample storage; it may look just like a mirror that's been hung on the wall. Surface-mounted cabinets, on the other hand, are more dominant visually. With either type, styles range from elaborately detailed to plain and simple in painted or natural wood or metal. In addition, specialty retailers and architectural salvage shops are a good source for period cabinets. Use your Web browser to look up "vintage medicine chests," for example, and you'll find everything from 1920s-era steel chests plated in brass, copper, or nickel to antique Chinese cabinets.

top right • This modern interpretation of a breakfront cabinet includes a trio of well-proportioned mirrors and cabinets, making a balanced as well as practical installation.

right • A surface-mounted medicine cabinet can add style to any space, and is one easy way to update a bathroom.

far right • This medicine chest installed in the wall has an added advantage: an open shelf on the bottom to use for additional storage or decorative accents.

Medicine cabinets set into the wall between studs are out of the way; when installed on an outside wall, though, this design means a loss of insulation.

Free-Standing Furniture

Pieces of furniture you're more accustomed to seeing in other parts of the house can be adapted for use in the bathroom, either as free-standing storage and shelving units or as vanities when fitted with countertops and sinks.

Think of the chest of drawers in the front hall where you normally store hats and mittens, the tall narrow bookcase in the basement, or your grandmother's buffet table gathering dust in the attic. All of them can be adapted to new uses in the bathroom. Simply talk to a local cabinet shop or woodworker to see if the piece can be adapted for use in the bathroom.

Manufacturers also are responding to greater interest in sink cabinets that look like furniture. They're less reliant on rectangular shapes than in the past, so you're sure to find cabinetry with curved shapes that will complement other fixtures and components in the bathroom.

top right and bottom right • A small bench doesn't take up much floor area but it makes a convenient place to sit or keep a towel or clothing while you shower.

above • Likely borrowed from another room in the house, this tapered open shelving unit makes an appealing addition to this formal bathroom.

Bringing a chest of drawers into the bathroom provides a generous amount of storage and makes the room feel homey and comfortable.

Open Storage

If you don't mind having your toiletries and other bathroom items out on display, open storage can be effective, particularly if you don't have a lot of space. Open shelving, for instance, is a great place to store rolled or stacked towels. Baskets, bins, and vintage containers are other good places to store not only towels but smaller toiletries, extra toilet paper, and anything you want to put your fingers on quickly. Be creative in your choice of container to impose your own flair and design style.

In really tight spaces where floor space is at a premium, make the most use of the walls by employing wall-mounted shelves, towel bars, hooks, and other hangers that offer a place to stow everything from an extra towel to your bathrobe, a hanging basket of lotions and cologne, or a sachet. Shaker-style peg boards are great for hanging damp towels or robes, and they take up no floor space.

top right • Baskets are inexpensive and make good-looking storage pieces. A unique touch for more storage: an old ladder turned into towel bar.

right • Simple storage cubbies between two enclosed cabinets make it easy to find a clean towel when you need one.

far right • Towel storage in the form of a simple rack on the back of the door takes up otherwise unused space.

Open shelving below this long vanity
top lightens the mass of the cabinet.

Storage Bins

Bathroom storage comes in many forms. A tray, a divided container, and even a galvanized pot all have found places in this bathroom. Using unrelated objects like these helps the bathroom seem personal and comfortable.

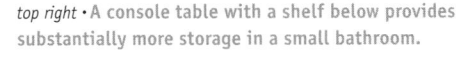

top right • A console table with a shelf below provides substantially more storage in a small bathroom.

above • Open shelves in the bathroom can display soft goods, which soak up noise that can bounce off hard surfaces.

left • An iron towel rack and a wire basket for magazines on top of the toilet tank complement the rustic texture of the wall tiles in this bathroom.

facing page • A shelf set on top of an old-fashioned cast iron radiator provides at least enough room for a few towels or a vase of flowers.

A Contemporary Blend

One thing that keeps this contemporary bathroom from looking cold or overly large is the introduction of warm wood surfaces—on the face of the long vanity cabinet, in the window muntins above the counter, and in the wall around the tub.

Details are subdued. Drawer and door pulls in the vanity, for example, are clearly visible but understated. The high wood wall by the tub is unadorned except for an incised grid pattern that helps give it some definition. A single band of bold blue is the one stroke of color the room really needs.

The shower design also helps the room feel spacious and open. Although the shower enclosure is fairly large, the frameless glass walls keep it from intruding in the space.

facing page • The edge of the backsplash surrounding the tub as well as the surround itself become shelving.

left • Because of its simple style and light above it, this conventional built-in doesn't look imposing, even though it's large enough to include 16 drawers and 2 enclosed cabinets.

bottom • A wide bench and a wall niche hold soap, shampoo, and other toiletries in the shower.

FINISHING

*With the major work out of the way, the time comes to make your
bathroom truly a reflection of your unique interests and tastes.*

TOUCHES

*From paint to potted plants, finishing touches add color, texture,
and variety, and imprint the room with your sense of style.*

Using color is one of the simplest and most economical ways to alter a bathroom's appearance. In a modest remodeling project, repainting the walls, ceiling, and even existing cabinets can make a bathroom look entirely different. Wallpaper, too, can be used to transform your bathroom without spending a lot of money, and because certain wallpapers come with a heavy backing they can also be helpful in fortifying cracked plaster or covering a not-so-great drywall-patching job.

The bathroom is also the perfect place to experiment with adding splashes of bold color and texture, because there isn't a lot of real estate to play with. Stained-or etched-glass panels over windows, a collection of framed prints, an interesting medicine chest, and myriad other accessories that can hang on the wall or from the ceiling can make your bathroom feel as warm and "designed" as the public spaces in your home.

DETAILS THAT WORK

The Fifth Wall

Ceilings are often forgotten zones, given a coat of flat white paint and then ignored. But think of the ceiling as the fifth wall, where an imaginative use of color, trim, or other decoration can enliven a room and give it character. Darker colors make the ceiling look closer; light colors give the illusion that it's farther away. Experiment, too, with trim to help break up the ceiling from the walls.

above • Intense color combined with a heavily textured stone counter don't feel overwhelming in this small bathroom because the homeowner rightly left the other details very simple.

right • Wallpaper has a long history as a wall finish, and manufacturers offer a variety of patterns, textures, and materials suitable for use in a bathroom. This pattern, teamed with a checkerboard mirror and detailed floor, is lively and fun.

A collection of framed prints with a theme dresses up this bathroom. But remember that bathrooms are often steamy environments and moisture may pose long-term risks for paper.

Paint

A basic design rule holds that dark colors make a room look smaller and more intimate, whereas lighter colors visually enlarge a space. This is a good place to start when thinking about what colors you want in your bathroom, but there's more to it than that. Dark colors can be successful even in small bathrooms when paired with a large mirrored surface—a full mirror behind the sink, for instance, or a mirror that entirely covers the back of a door—and lots of light. The effect is one of intimacy without inducing claustrophobia.

Color is a highly personal choice—one person's bilious green is another's delightful lime. But along with the kind of lighting that's used in the bathroom, color has a pronounced effect on how we look in the mirror. Yellows and greens, for example, have a way of making us look sickly even when we're feeling fine. Your skin tones may look best with cool blues, warm reds, or a neutral peach. How to tell? Start with the color of a favorite sweater or shirt—the one you always think you look good in—and wrap the walls in it. If down the road you decide you want an entirely different color it won't be hard to change.

Bolder wall colors also can be very effective when used on one or two walls instead of an entire room. A warm terracotta or a deep green will contrast nicely with an off-white on adjacent walls, for example, making the room more interesting without overwhelming it.

right · To help keep this bathroom quiet in tone and a place of rest, plants and simple artwork were chosen as the decorative accents.

Paint That Tricks the Eye

Commissioning an artist to paint a mural or *trompe l'oeil*, a French term that means "to fool the eye," is one way of achieving a bathroom wall finish that's completely unique. In this bathroom the artist worked with outdoor imagery as well as the homeowners' favorite themes—doves, a pond, and children modeled after their own grandchildren playing in a garden.

The artist used colors that complement other features in the room: A blue sky above the tub harmonizes with the blue tile in the shower and on the tub surround. The high ceiling in the room, illuminated by a skylight, also works with the theme of the painting, the height suggesting the openness of the sky. In all, elements of the room have been chosen carefully to complement each other and enhance the effect of being in a pleasant outdoor space.

top right • This decorative wall painting, commissioned from a local artist, includes clouds and a few shoots of ivy on the wall over the tub.

right • The French term for a painting that fools the eye is *trompe l'oeil,* and here it enlivens a long stretch of wall with an outdoor scene.

Paint

Choosing paint color is just a first step. You'll also have to consider whether you want oil or latex paint and what surface sheen will look best in the room.

OIL PAINT

- Typically used on baseboard and door and window trim.
- Contains volatile organic compounds, chemicals that affect some people adversely and are now under increasingly tighter government control.
- Odor may last for days as paint cures.
- Flows out to form smooth, hard surface.
- Dries slowly.
- Cleans up with solvents.

LATEX PAINT

- Dries quickly.
- Fewer noxious chemicals and less odor than oil paint.
- Cleans up with water.
- Paints with higher proportion of acrylic latex are more durable.

SHEEN

- Describes the reflectivity of the paint.
- Most paints come in a range of sheens, from flat (no sheen) to gloss (high sheen). Intermediate steps include eggshell or satin and semigloss.
- Gloss and semigloss are conventionally used on surfaces that need periodic scrubbing, although flat paints that can be scrubbed also are available. Consult your paint dealer.
- High-gloss paints show more surface defects; flat paint is better for concealing them.
- Both oil and latex paints come in the same variety of sheens.

Contrasting sharply with the dark wood of the cabinets and wainscoting, the bold diagonal pattern on the walls gives this bathroom vitality.

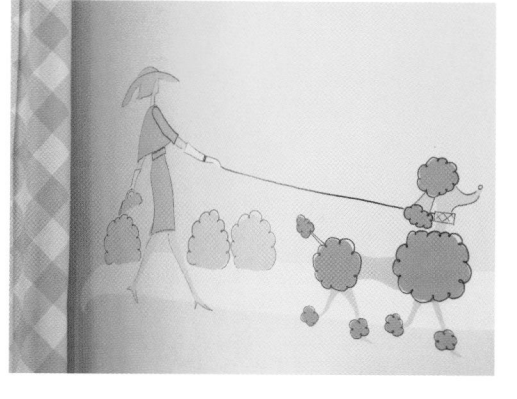

left · Even a small detail can make all the difference. This French-style scene is perfect in a woman's bath.

bottom · This beautiful glass console sink would have really stood out if the walls in this bathroom were white, but the aquamarine walls in nearly the same shade make the bathroom feel balanced and peaceful.

The Power of Color

Sometimes a bold color choice is successful when it's used only sparingly. The intense blue of this tile border electrifies this bathroom mainly because the rest of the room is predominantly white. The stainless steel of the sink and the few wooden surfaces also are more dramatic because of that contrast. Running the tile border around the room helps to draw the design together, as does a similar blue border in the floor.

Keeping to a two-color main theme still allowed other colors to be brought into the room subtly. The huge expanse of window over the tub means that nature—and all its beautiful colors—are featured in the room year-round.

right • Dense foliage outside the bathroom makes its own color contribution to the room.

facing page top • Carrying the blue border right through the shower helps connect it with the rest of the room.

facing page bottom • The power of color in this bathroom is its near absence. A band of blue marking the top of the tile wainscoting is all the more dramatic because there is so little color elsewhere.

Wallpaper

Some designers think the sun has set on wallpaper as an appealing form of wall decoration, but there are plenty who'd disagree. Like anything else involving décor, it's simply a matter of personal preference.

Some types of wallpaper are suitable in high-humidity bathrooms. Hundreds of patterns and colors can be found in cloth, paper-backed vinyl, vinyl-coated paper, nonwoven material, silk, and plain old paper.

There are plenty of specialized types of wallpaper, too, including thicker commercial grades of vinyl that can help protect wall surfaces in a bathroom used by children and nonwoven varieties that are similar to those indestructible envelopes used by Federal Express that neither stretch nor tear. In bathrooms with cracked plaster walls, special reinforcing wallpaper can hide cosmetic defects and strengthen damaged surfaces when it's not practical to tear out the old plaster and replace it. These wallpapers come with different weaves, and some of them can even be painted.

Although bathrooms with frequently used showers may need to be covered in a vinyl wallpaper for durability, powder rooms can feature a more delicate, high-impact wallpaper such as silk or grass cloth.

Buy an Extra Roll

If you opt for wallpaper, buy an extra roll and tuck it away. In the event that a wall is damaged, having the paper on hand means you won't be trying to track down a pattern that's no longer available. Paper ordered at the same time should carry the same lot number, an assurance that colors and patterns will match. A few years later that might not be possible.

This vibrant blue wallpaper sets the stage for a beautiful vanity cabinet and concrete countertop. All accessories blend so as not to detract from the focal points of the room.

facing page, top • Wallpaper can be customized to fit the personality of the bathroom's occupants; the brothers who share this bathroom drew the lizard scene that was then made into wallpaper.

facing page, bottom • If you're looking for only a spot of color, consider a wallpaper border. This is also a good idea for a kids' bathroom that you might want to update easily when the kids grow up.

top • A subdued floral pattern gives this bathroom a faintly nostalgic feel.

bottom • This blue-patterned paper has added impact when paired with bead board wainscoting in a neutral color.

top • Louvered shutters covering the bottom of the window ensure privacy for anyone in the tub, but leaving the upper part of the window uncovered allows in more light and the only other color evidenced in the room.

above • A sheer white fabric roller shade doesn't detract from the splashes of color used in this room. Fabric offers a touch of femininity.

Window Coverings

Nowhere in the house is a window covering more important than in a bathroom. After all, this is one room where privacy is essential. But that doesn't mean your bathroom needs to be a fortress. Window coverings can be practical and stylish, and by layering multiple types of treatments you can have a well-designed window that doesn't need to be dismantled every time you want to take a leisurely soak in the tub.

As with other decorating elements, your choice of fabric, pattern, color, and style depends on what you want to accomplish and how you want the window treatment to interact with the rest of the bathroom. Color can be used to blend or make a statement, but it's good to know that solids and small-print fabrics work well on just about any window, whereas large prints are better on windows that are also large in scale. Styles range from valances to Roman shades, plantation shutters to swags and balloon shades. New choices in hardware, tiebacks, and embellishments mean that you can personalize even the most simple of window treatments.

top left · Valances let in as much natural light as possible. For privacy, roller shades can be installed underneath them.

left · Shirred half-curtains on this pair of windows offer just the right amount of privacy over the tub enclosure. The all-white bathroom radiates with sunshine from the bare upper half of the windows.

facing page · Layered window treatments can be especially effective in a bathroom, because one layer, here the side panels, can remain stationary while the other, in this case the Roman shades, can be dropped for privacy.

Details

There are a variety of other elements that can help you put your personal stamp on your bathroom. Potted plants, small pieces of sculpture, framed artwork, fabric shower curtains, and even the door and window trim all play a part in creating the room you want.

The high moisture levels you'd expect to find in a bathroom will help some plants thrive. For bathrooms with lots of light, consider flowering houseplants such as hibiscus. In darker bathrooms, ferns are a better bet. Cactus and succulents tend to like drier environments, making them better candidates for a powder room than a bathroom where a shower is used several times a day.

Prints, paintings, and other artwork hanging on the wall can help establish a consistent theme in a bathroom—but moisture is a key consideration. Paper is an organic material, and excessive moisture may lead to the growth of mold, damaging or ruining the work. In bathrooms where water gets splashed frequently or long, steamy showers are the norm, look for other ways of decorating walls. But in powder rooms and other low-impact bathrooms, framed prints or photographs are a terrific way of personalizing the space and adding visual variety.

Shower curtains and throw rugs also can be used to introduce a burst of color. Woven cotton rugs are naturally absorbent, warm underfoot, easy to launder, and inexpensive enough to replace periodically without breaking the bank.

top right • Plants help absorb noise and add color and texture. Be sure to choose those well adapted to a bathroom environment of high humidity and typically not much natural light.

right • The formal yet simple accessories on this vanity top fit the feel of the bathroom and are a good example of accents taking a backseat to beautiful fixtures and materials.

top • Framed prints can create or enhance a theme in the bathroom. Here an orderly row of fern prints introduce a back-to-nature theme.

above • A garland of tin flowers encircles the handcrafted mirror in this New Mexico house, sized perfectly to fit over the backsplash.

left • Colored tiles, sunflower wallpaper, and plaid shower curtain combine well because they feature shades of the same color families.

Subtle Detailing

This first-floor bath in a house on Bainbridge Island, Wash., is a model of subtle detailing. Starting with a nearly 9-ft. ceiling in the 1920s-era cottage-style house, the architect added a curved dropped ceiling of 1x4 tongue-and-groove cedar to improve the proportions of the room and hide the ceiling-mounted exhaust fan. Air is drawn through the ceiling with the help of slots cut into the ceiling boards.

Because the room is used only occasionally as a guest bath, the architect did away with the shower enclosure to make the room seem larger and more open. A hand-held shower ensures the bath is still functional.

New materials include the wainscoting of blue glass tile, a major expense, and a cork floor. A new pedestal sink takes the place of a cumbersome vanity, and a new cabinet at the foot of the tub provides storage for towels.

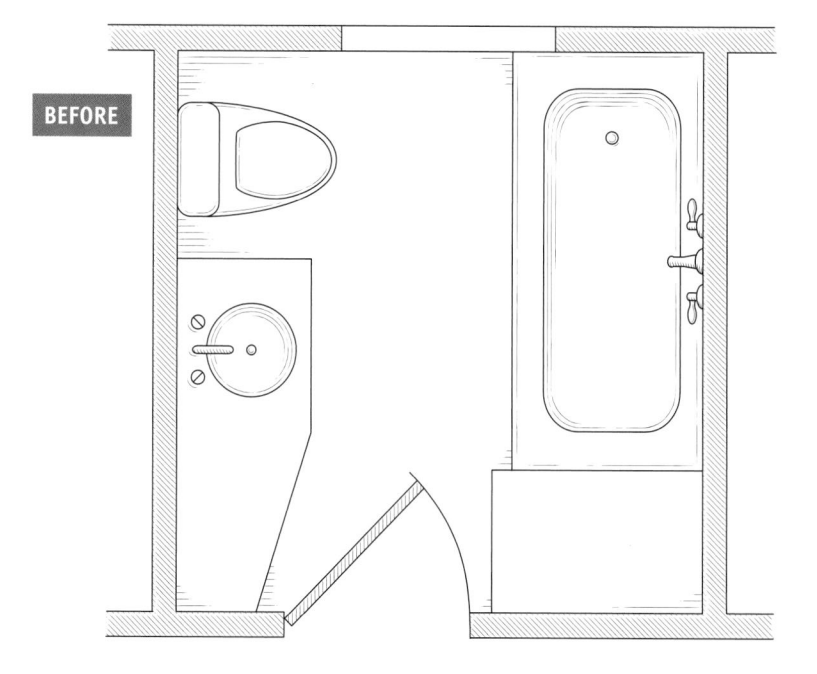

BEFORE

Making More Room

Bath fixtures stayed in place, lowering the cost of the project, but two changes make the room feel more spacious. A conventional sink vanity was replaced by a pedestal sink, and a pocket door was swapped for the conventional swinging door.

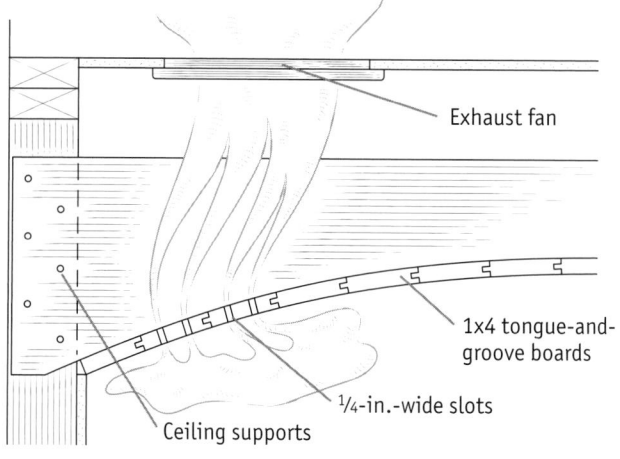

Exhaust fan

1x4 tongue-and-groove boards

¼-in.-wide slots

Ceiling supports

Lowering the Ceiling

Curved supports cut from 2x12 lumber lie behind the pleasantly arched ceiling. Slots cut in the 1x4 tongue-and-groove cedar boards allow exhaust air to be vented upward without the usual fan grille on the ceiling.

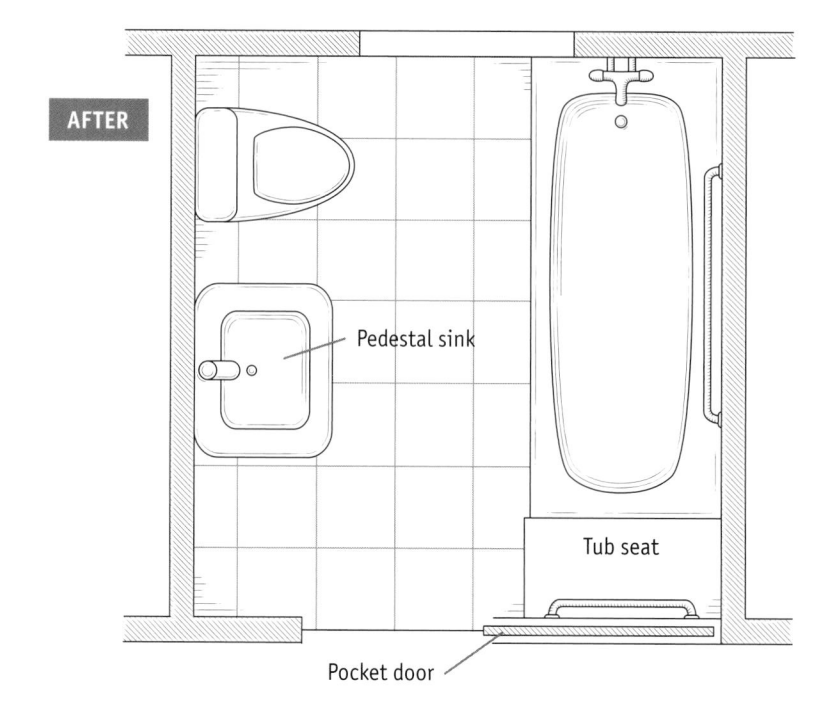

AFTER

Pedestal sink

Tub seat

Pocket door

Tongue-and-groove cedar boards attached to curved supports made from dimensional lumber lower the 9-ft. ceiling and bring better proportions to this small bathroom. Exhaust air is drawn through slots cut into the boards.

RESOURCES

Organizations and Associations

**CENTER FOR
UNIVERSAL DESIGN**
North Carolina
State University
919-515-3082
www.design.ncsu.edu/cud

**INTERNATIONAL
CAST POLYMER ALLIANCE**
703-525-0511
www.icpa-hq.org

**MARBLE INSTITUTE
OF AMERICA**
440-250-9222
www.marble-institute.com

**NATIONAL ASSOCIATION
OF HOME BUILDERS**
800-368-5242
www.nahb.org

**NATIONAL KITCHEN
AND BATH ASSOCIATION**
800-843-6522
www.nkba.com

**TILE COUNCIL
OF NORTH AMERICA**
864-646-8453
www.tileusa.com

Manufacturers and Suppliers

ADAGIO
561-988-2297
www.adagiosinks.com
Sinks

AMERICAN STANDARD
800-442-1902
www.americanstandard-us.com
Plumbing fixtures

BROAN-NUTONE
800-445-6057
www.broan-nutone.com
Ventilation equipment

CHICAGO FAUCET
847-803-5000
www.chicagofaucets.com
Faucets

DELTA FAUCET CO.
800-345-3358
www.deltafaucet.com
Faucets

ELJER MANUFACTURING CO.
800-423-5537
www.eljer.com
Plumbing fixtures

FANTECH
800-747-1762
www.fantech.net
Ventilation equipment

GROHE FAUCETS
630-582-7711
www.groheamerica.com
Faucets

JACUZZI WHIRLPOOL BATH
800-288-4402
www.jacuzzi.com
Whirlpool bathtubs

KEIDEL SUPPLY CO.
513-351-1600
www.keidel.com
*Fixtures and faucets
with excellent background
material on website*

KOHLER CO.
800-456-4537
www.kohler.com
Plumbing fixtures

**MANSFIELD
PLUMBING PRODUCTS**
903-657-1436
www.mansfieldplumbing.com
Plumbing fixtures

MTI WHIRLPOOLS
800-783-8827
www.mtiwhirlpools.com
Whirlpool bathtubs

MYSON INC.
800-698-9690
www.mysoninc.com
Towel warmers

PANASONIC
201-392-6169
www.panasonic.com
Ventilation equipment

PORCHER
800-359-3261
www.porcher-us.com
Plumbing fixtures

RUNTAL NORTH AMERICA
800-526-2621
www.runtalnorthamerica.com
Heated towel bars

SANIFLO INC.
800-363-5874
www.saniflo.com
Macerating toilets

TOTO
770-282-8696
www.totousa.com
Plumbing fixtures.

VICTORIA + ALBERT
866-850-0433
www.englishtubs.com
Soaking tubs

p. 66: Left: © Mark Lohman; design: Lynn Pries Design; right: © The Taunton Press, Inc.

p. 67: Left: © Brian Vanden Brink, Photographer 2006; design: Sholz & Barclay Architects; right: © Mark Lohman; design: Janet Lohman Design

p. 68: Top: © Brian Vanden Brink, Photographer 2006; design: John Silverio, Architect; bottom: Courtesy Porcher

p. 69: © Brian Vanden Brink, Photographer 2006

p. 70: © Brian Vanden Brink, Photographer 2006; design: Shope Reno Wharton Architects

p. 72: Top: © Brian Vanden Brink, Photographer 2006; bottom: © Brian Vanden Brink, Photographer 2006; design: Tom Catalano, Architect

p. 73: © Rob Karosis; design: Dan Wheeler, Architect

p. 74: Top: © Brian Vanden Brink, Photographer 2006; design: Stephen Blatt Architects; bottom: © Brian Vanden Brink, Photographer 2006; design: John Colomarino, Architect; left: Todd Caverly, © Brian Vanden Brink, Photographer 2006; design: Whipple Calendar Architects

p. 75: © Brian Vanden Brink, Photographer 2006; design: Siemasko & Verbridge Architects

p. 76: © Brian Vanden Brink, Photographer 2006

p. 77: © Brian Vanden Brink, Photographer 2006

p. 78: © Eric Roth; design: Duffy Design Group

p. 79: Top: © Brian Vanden Brink, Photographer 2006; design: John Morris, Architect; bottom: © Eric Roth; design: Siemasko + Verbridge Architects

p. 80: © Mark Lohman; design: Kyser Interiors

p. 81: Top: Courtesy MTI Whirlpool; bottom: © Brian Vanden Brink, Photographer 2006; design: Siemasko & Verbridge Architects; right: © Brian Vanden Brink, Photographer 2006; design: John Morris, Architect

p. 82: Left: Courtesy Victoria + Albert; top: © Anne Gummerson; design: Faith

Nevins; bottom: © Olson Photographic; design: Sally Scott, Sally Scott Interior Design

p. 83: © Mark Lohman

p. 84: © Alan Geller

p. 85: Top: © Mark Lohman; bottom: Courtesy Victoria + Albert

p. 86: Left: © Brian Vanden Brink, Photographer 2006; right: © Mark Lohman

p. 87: Top left: © Brian Vanden Brink, Photographer 2006; top right: © Brian Vanden Brink, Photographer 2006; design: Morningstar Marble & Granite; bottom: © Eric Roth; design: Laura Glen

p. 88: Top left: © Mark Lohman; top right: © Brian Vanden Brink, Photographer 2006; design: Alex Berg Builder; bottom: © Rob Karosis; design: Richard Brown, Architect

p. 89: © Brian Vanden Brink, Photographer 2006; design: Dominic Marcadante, Architect

p. 90: © Rob Karosis; design: Gary Milici, Architect

p. 91: Top: © Mark Lohman; design: Roxanne Packham Design and Michele Hughes Design; bottom left: © Brian Vanden Brink, Photographer 2006; design: G.M. Wild Construction, Inc.; bottom right: © Brian Vanden Brink, Photographer 2006

p. 92: Courtesy Karol Kurth Architects

p. 93: © Barry Halkin

p. 94: Left: © Eric Roth; design: Susan Sargent Design

pp. 94-95: © Anne Gummerson; design: Su-Lin Interiors

p. 95: Top: © Brian Vanden Brink, Photographer 2006; bottom: © Brian Vanden Brink, Photographer 2006; design: John Morris, Architect

p. 96: Left: © Mark Lohman; right: © Mark Lohman; design: S. Phillipps Design

p. 97: Courtesy Kohler

p. 98: Left © Eric Roth; design: Tile Showcase; top right: © Mark Lohman; design: Lotto Design Group; bottom right: Courtesy Kohler

p. 99: Top left: © Eric Roth; top middle: © Eric Roth; design: Tile Showcase; top right: Courtesy Kohler; bottom left: © Brian Vanden Brink, Photographer 2006; design: Sholz & Barclay Architects; bottom middle: Courtesy Kohler; bottom right: © Mark Lohman

p. 100: Courtesy Carol Kurth Architects

p. 101: Top: © Rob Karosis; design: Geoffrey Warner, Architect; bottom: © Olson Photographic; design: Nancy Budd, Budd Interiors; right: © Anne Gummerson, design: Alex Baer Design

p. 102: © Timothy Gill

p. 103: © The Taunton Press, Inc.

p. 104: © Mark Lohman

p. 106: © Mark Lohman; design: Burdge & Associates

p. 107: Top left: © Anne Gummerson; top right: © Eric Roth; design: Laura Langworthy Interior Design; bottom: © Rob Karosis; design: Barbara Winslow, Architect

p. 108: Left: © Eric Roth; design: Kathleen Sullivan Elliot; right photos: © Joseph Kugielsky

p. 109: Photos © Joseph Kugielsky

p. 110: Left: © Eric Roth; design: Tile Showcase; top: © Eric Roth; bottom: © Eric Roth, design: Dennis Duffy, Duffy Design Group

p. 111: © Brian Vanden Brink, Photographer 2006

pp. 112-113: © The Taunton Press, Inc.

p. 113: © The Taunton Press, Inc.

p. 114: Left: © Alise O'Brien; design: Directions in Design; top right: © Olson Photographic; design: Simon Johnson, Northeast Cabinet Design; bottom right: © Eric Roth

p. 115: © Olson Photographic; design: Heather McWilliam, McWilliam-Autore Interiors

p. 116: Top left: © Eric Roth, design: Ned Jalbert Interior Design; top right: © Eric Roth, design: Kathleen Sullivan Elliot; bottom: © Rob Karosis, design: David Brown, Architect

p. 117: © Mark Lohman, design: Burdge and Associates

p. 118: Top: Courtesy Armstrong; bottom: Courtesy Formica

p. 119: Left: Courtesy Mannington Mills; top right: Courtesy Formica; bottom right: Courtesy Mannington Mills

pp. 120-121: © The Taunton Press, Inc.

p. 121: Top: © Alan Geller; bottom: © Mark Lohman; design: Lynn Pries Design

p. 122: Left: © Eric Roth; design: Dennis Duffy, Duffy Design Group; top and bottom: © Brian Vanden Brink, Photographer 2006

p. 123: © Barry Halkin

p. 124: Top: Courtesy Carol Kurth Architects; bottom: © Rob Karosis; design: Lane Williams, Architect

p. 125: © Eric Roth; design: Susan Sargent Designs

p. 126: © Brian Vanden Brink, Photographer 2006

p. 127: Left: © Brian Vanden Brink, Photo-grapher 2006; design: Dominic Mercadante, Architect; right: © Anne Gummerson

p. 128: Top: © Brian Vanden Brink, Photographer 2006; design: Elliot Elliot Norelius Architects; left © Eric Roth; design: Marcus Gleysteen, Architect; top and bottom middle: © Eric Roth; design: Tile Showcase; right: © Eric Roth

p. 129: © Mark Lohman; design: Kathryn Designs

p. 130: Left: © Alise O'Brien; design: Colleen Horner Kitchen Bath Tile Stone; top: courtesy: Carol Kurth Architects; bottom: Courtesy Hamilton-Grey Design

p. 131: © Eric Roth; design: Laura Langworthy

p. 132: © Mark Lohman; design: Lynn Pries Design

p. 133: Top left: © Eric Roth; design: Molly Moran, Architect; top right: © Eric Roth; bottom: © Olson Photographic; design: Betsy House, Kitchen and Bath Designs

pp. 134–135: Photos © Olson Photographic; design: Joe Currie, Currie Design Associates

p. 136: Courtesy Belanger Clement

p. 138: Top left: Courtesy Belanger Clement Olson Photographic; design: Andrew Payne, Benchmark Builders/

Jean Marie McLaughlin, Jmac & Kennedy; top right: Courtesy Carol Kurth Architects; bottom: © Brian Vanden Brink, Photographer 2006; design: Stephen Blatt, Architect

p. 139: © Brian Vanden Brink, Photographer 2006; design: Sholz & Barclay Architects

p. 140: © Eric Roth

p. 141: © Brian Vanden Brink, Photographer 2006

p. 142: Photo by Todd Caverly, © Brian Vanden Brink, Photographer 2006; design: George Snead J.R., Interior Design

p. 143: © Brian Vanden Brink, Photographer 2006

p. 144: © Anne Gummerson; design: Andre Fontaine

p. 145: Top: photo by Todd Caverly, © Brian Vanden Brink, Photographer 2006; design: G.M. Wild Construction, Inc.; bottom left: © Brian Vanden Brink, Photographer 2006; design: John Morris, Architect; bottom right: © Brian Vanden Brink, Photographer 2006; design: Morningstar Marble & Granite

p. 146: Photos © Rob Karosis; design: Geoffrey Warner, Architect

p. 147: Left: © The Taunton Press, Inc.; right: © Olson Photographic; design: Joe Currie, Currie Design Associates

p. 148: Top left: © Brian Vanden Brink, Photographer 2006; top right: Courtesy Carol Kurth Architects; bottom: © Rob Karosis; design: Dwight McNeil, Architect

p. 149: © Brian Vanden Brink, Photographer 2006

p. 150: Left: © Brian Vanden Brink, Photographer 2006; design: Scholz & Barclay Architects; top right: © Mark Lohman; bottom right: © Mark Lohman, design: Lynn Pries Design

p. 151: © Mark Lohman

p. 152: © Eric Roth

p. 154: Left: © Brian Vanden Brink, Photographer 2006; design: Elliot Elliot Norelius Architects; top: © Brian Vanden Brink, Photographer 2006; bottom: © Brian Vanden Brink, Photographer 2006; design: Brett Donham Architect

p. 155: © Brian Vanden Brink, Photographer 2006; design: Sally Weston, Architect

p. 156: Left: © Brian Vanden Brink, Photographer 2006; right: Courtesy Carol Kurth Architects

p. 157: Photos courtesy Carol Kurth Architects

pp. 158-159: © Brian Vanden Brink, Photographer 2006; design: Io Oakes Interior Design

p. 159: Courtesy Broan-Nutone

p. 160: © Brian Vanden Brink, Photographer 2006

p. 161: © Mark Lohman

p. 162: Left: © Barry Halkin; right: © Eric Roth

p. 163: Left: © Rob Karosis; right: © Brian Vanden Brink, Photographer 2006

p. 164: Photo by Todd Caverly, © Brian Vanden Brink, Photographer 2006; design: G.M. Wild Construction, Inc.

p. 165: © Olson Photographic, design: Geri Russell, Cross Key Designs

p. 166: © Anne Gummerson

p. 168: Left: © Brian Vanden Brink, Photographer 2006; design: John Cole, Architect; top: © Brian Vanden Brink, Photographer 2006; bottom: © Anne Gummerson

p. 169: © Barry Halkin

p. 170: © Mark Samu

p. 171: Top left: © Brian Vanden Brink, Photographer 2006; top right: © Mark Samu; bottom: © Rob Karosis; design: Pi Smith, Architect

p. 172: Top: © Olson Photographic; design: Sally Scott, Sally Scott Interior Design; bottom: © Eric Roth; design: Michael Weiss Interior Dimensions

p. 173: © Eric Roth, design: Paul White, Weena and Spook

p. 174: Left: © Olson Photographic; design: Anthony Totilo, Anthony Totilo Architects; top right: © Alan Geller; bottom right: © Olson Photographic; design: Joe Currie, Currie Design Associates

p. 175: © Alan Geller

p. 176: © Brian Vanden Brink, Photographer 2006; design: Christina Oliver I.D.

p. 177: Top: © Eric Roth; design: Gregor Cann; bottom: © Mark Lohman, design Kathryne Designs

p. 178: Left: © Olson Photographic; design: Sally Scott, Sally Scott Interior Design; top right: © Mark Lohman; bottom right: © Adolfo Perez

p. 179: © Olson Photographic; design: Sally Scott, Sally Scott Interior Design

p. 180: Left: © Barry Halkin; top right: © Brian Vanden Brink, Photographer 2006; design: John Colomarino, Architect; bottom right: © Mark Lohman

p. 181: Top left: © Mark Lohman; design: Roxanne Packham Design and Michele Hughes Design; bottom left: © Anne Gummerson, design: Brennan Associates; right: © Brian Vanden Brink, Photographer 2006; design: Christina Oliver I.D.

p. 183: © Art Grice

p. 184: Top: © Mark Lohman; bottom left: Photo by Todd Caverly, © Brian Vanden Brink, Photographer 2006; design: G.M. Wild Construction, Inc.; bottom right: © Eric Roth; design: Heather Wells, Architect

p. 185: © Brian Vanden Brink, Photographer 2006; design: Elliot Elliot Norelius Architects

p. 186: Left: © Anne Gummerson; design: Alex Baer Design; top right: © Brian Vanden Brink, Photographer 2006; design: Bernhard & Priestly Architects; bottom right: © Rob Karosis; design: Ken Dahlin, Architect

p. 187: © Mark Lohman

p. 188: Top: © Alise O'Brien, design: brooksBerry; bottom left: © Brian Vanden Brink, Photographer 2006; bottom right: © Brian Vanden Brink, Photographer 2006; design: South Mountain Company Builders

p. 189: © Brian Vanden Brink, Photographer 2006

p. 190: © Anne Gummerson; design: Brennen Associates

p. 191: Top left: © Mark Lohman; design: Cynthia Marks Design; top right: © Olson Photographic; design: Heather McWilliam, McWilliam-Autore Interiors; bottom left and right: © Eric Roth

pp. 192-193: © Mark Lohman; design: Abramson Tieger

p. 194: © Eric Roth; design: David Stirling, Architects

p. 196: Left: © Eric Roth; top right: © Olson Photographic, design: Sally Scott, Sally Scott Interior Design; bottom right: © Eric Roth, design: David Stirling, Architect

p. 197: © Eric Roth

p. 198: © Mark Lohman

p. 199: Photos Alise O'Brien; design: Directions in Design

pp. 200-201: © Eric Roth; design: Ned Jalbert Interior Design

p. 201: Top: © Eric Roth; bottom: © Anne Gummerson; design: Gilday Design-Build

pp. 202-203: © Mark Lohman; design: Kanner Architects

p. 204: Top: © Douglas Salin; bottom: Courtesy York Wall Coverings

p. 205: Left: © Roger Turk/Northlight Photographer; top and bottom right: © Eric Roth

p. 206: Top left: © Brian Vanden Brink, Photographer 2006; Elliot Elliot Norelius Architects; bottom left: © Phillip Ennis; right: © Tim Street-Porter

p. 207: Top: © Brian Vanden Brink, Photographer 2006; design: Drysdale Associates I.D.; bottom: © The Taunton Press, Inc.

p. 208: Top: © Rob Karosis; design: Ken Dahlin, Architect; bottom: © Mark Lohman; design: Burdge and Associates

p. 209: Left: © Wendell Weber; top right: © Brian Vanden Brink, Photographer 2006; bottom right: © Rob Karosis; design: Georgia Hoffman, Designer

p. 211: © Art Grice

INDEX